HOW DO YC
ARE MAKIN(

MW00638676

A Practical Handbook for Public Service Organisations

Sarah Morton and Ailsa Cook

P

First published in Great Britain in 2023 by

Policy Press, an imprint of
Bristol University Press
University of Bristol
1–9 Old Park Hill
Bristol
BS2 8BB
UK
t: +44 (0)117 374 6645
e: bup-info@bristol.ac.uk

Details of international sales and distribution partners are available at
policy.bristoluniversitypress.co.uk

British Library Cataloguing in Publication Data
A catalogue record for this book is available from the British Library

ISBN 978-1-4473-6193-0 paperback
ISBN 978-1-4473-6194-7 ePub
ISBN 978-1-4473-6195-4 ePdf

Cover design: Hayes Design and Advertising

We dedicate this book to:

Sarah's father, Richard Morton who taught her to look for the evidence behind any claim.

And Ailsa's daughter, Esther, who asks the best questions.

Contents

List of figures and tables

Figures

Tables

Acknowledgements

There are many people who have helped make this book a reality. Our lovely team members at Matter of Focus have helped by supporting us to develop this approach and reviewing the work: Charlie Mills has been our internal editor, Kathleen Taylor proofread, helped with case studies and compiled references, and Alex Perry has done some wonderful work to make the diagrams and tables look good and assisted with proofreading. All of our clients since we set up Matter of Focus in 2017 have helped in developing this approach, and we particularly want to thank those that have agreed to let us highlight their work in these pages. A special thanks to Leah Black from WHALE Arts who coined the term 'owning your outcomes' that we have built on in this text. Thanks to the Policy Press for commissioning this, and for their support through the process. Thanks to Yasmin Yarwood for professional copy-editing and proofreading. Finally, thanks to our families who have had to put up with our obsession with impact, outcomes and evidence, and have given us the time and space to write a book and run a business through the pandemic.

Preface

Thank you for picking up this book. We want to set the scene in this preface by explaining why we wanted to write it; that is, how we met, what we both brought with us and how that was developed through working together on one of our early projects. We have used a fictionalised version of the project we introduce here throughout the rest of the book as an example. It explains why it's often hard to demonstrate impact.

It started when we met through our connections with the University of Edinburgh. Ailsa had been working in the personal outcomes space, leading a master's programme for health and social care managers and a programme of action research exploring meaningful and measurable outcome recording and assessment. Sarah was working in the research and evidence to action space, working with organisations to use research and evidence to drive change, and developing understanding through research and practical projects about what evidence use looks like in the real world. What we shared was a commitment to using our skills to make a difference to the problems we saw organisations facing, and to bringing robust academic thinking to very practical issues. We have come to consider ourselves practical academics – pracademics!

In particular, Ailsa was acutely aware that organisations in health and social care were troubled by the issues of meaningfully assessing outcomes, and Sarah had been experimenting with contribution analysis as a way of understanding research impact and wider change processes. Once we started talking about bringing these two issues together, and trying it out with some of our projects, we could really see the potential. We started working together in 2014 and set up our company, Matter of Focus, in 2017 as a vehicle to develop the approach, bring it to more people and create tools to make it genuinely practical for organisations to use. We want to tell you about one of our early projects together as a way of illustrating the issues that we help teams to face.

In the first year of our company, we worked with a local wellbeing service that assisted people through a personal outcomes approach – defining with people what was important to them and encouraging them towards their own goals. This service was doing all the things seen as appropriate in current thinking: taking an asset-based approach, being outcome focused and developing a preventative service. People running this service saw great transformation in people's lives. People using the service also reported how much it helped them. Everyone thought they were reaching people otherwise not getting a service, and the local GP services were really impressed and keen to develop and extend the work.

But despite all this good news, the service was under threat. It had been funded with one-off investment from money for transforming primary care. To continue, the service needed to make the case to the Health and Social Care Partnership and GP practices and demonstrate that it was making the desired difference. Despite having lots of expertise in data and evidence, the team were finding this hard to do. The usual approaches to evidencing how good the service was and its value for money were both hard to implement and didn't reflect the difference everyone could see on the ground.

The service sat across health and social care and so faced being judged in two ways: by a set of standards developed for clinical interventions and adapted for use in public health, and by the local authority on best value and accountability in public service. These two subtly different ways of thinking and measuring sat uneasily with the service. These were the expected ways of doing things, and while decision makers weren't wedded to these approaches to demonstrating impact, this is what they were used to, and what their systems were built around.

What was wrong with these existing ways of understanding and measuring change? The public service system homed in on delivering outcomes and reducing costs. Targets were set for the local Health and Social Care Partnership to be judged against, so it was easiest to invest in services that contributed most directly to these targets. This service was upstream and preventative and therefore didn't directly contribute to targets that were more about key areas of stress in the system, such as reducing admissions to hospital, with constant pressures on budgets. While officially interested in preventative work, there are difficulties in funding it in the short term because providing services to people who had been excluded increases immediate costs. Further down the line, their health and wellbeing would improve and they would be less likely to need acute services, but unless there was a longer-term budgeting vision on reducing costs, this would not help.

It was also hard to evidence benefits through a health improvement lens. Public health seeks to identify effective interventions that can be rolled out more widely, so the drive is to prove impacts using approaches developed for clinical trials. That means counting interventions, ensuring fidelity to interventions and then counting outcomes. Doing this for a tailored personal outcome service is almost impossible as outcomes can't be set, nor easily aggregated when they are tailored to each person using the service. It was appropriate to deliver for each person in the way they needed – that's what was at the heart of this approach. It was not about how many appointments, but the quality of the conversation and ongoing support – things that are much less easily measurable or captured in standard indicators established to show fidelity to a process.

Some of these types of measures had been agreed when the service was established but practitioners found them frustrating – they felt they were 'feeding the machine' and the measures didn't get meaningful information but took up precious time and resources to record the data and ensure consistency. We have seen this many times in our work – the reporting requirements just don't fit the work being done. Here, staff felt that some questionnaires were deficit led and demeaning, and cut across their asset-based approach. They felt that getting before and after measures got in the way of what they knew to be good practice in delivering a person-centred service. They could see that how people they supported felt about outcomes changed over time; they would often score themselves lower as trust developed and they gained insight into themselves and what they wanted in life.

Our approach, the one set out in this book, offered this service a different way of doing things. We worked together over six months to embed an alternative impact assessment approach that was more aligned to the work being done. The approach to cause and effect was appropriate to the work in hand; that is, it recognised the complex and relational nature of this service. We co-created an outcome map that put relationships at the heart of change. Together, we defined and discussed the complexity of this kind of service delivery, recognising and acknowledging the risks and assumptions that underpinned the work. We supported them to interrogate and reflect on the data and information they had already captured about the service, and to stop collecting data that wasn't helping them learn or understand change. We identified new ways of collecting more qualitative data that could meaningfully supplement their understanding. We developed space for sense-making by bringing this together to understand and report on the difference the service made, what was going well and where they could learn. Because this approach fitted the work being done, it created a compelling contribution story that the funders were happy to accept as an alternative way of reporting on this work.

All of our work since then has had similar themes: projects, teams and organisations who value relationship-based ways of working to tackle complex problems, and often taking asset-based, collaborative approaches, innovating new ways of doing things and focusing on prevention. They sense that numbers don't tell the story but lack alternative ways of working. They need to make the case for what they do and want methods that back what matters to them and the people they work with. Often, they feel they have to 'feed the machine' with numbers, categories and data that seem meaningless, generally a waste of time and sometimes destructive.

Our journey in establishing a practical but robust way of understanding if you're making a difference has been honed through work with many projects like these over the last five years, along with the development of a software product that upholds this way of doing things. We wanted people to have an alternative to numbers-based software – something meaningful, and even fun to use, that championed learning and reflection. It has been a steep learning curve for us, but we are now officially tech entrepreneurs as well as pracademics! We are proud to have created something that helps people use qualitative and mixed data well in this difficult and challenging work.

If you see elements of your own work in the service described above, or you have faced any of the challenges we have outlined, this book is for you! If you are interested in how we develop a wider range of approaches to making a difference – making the best difference possible – and being able to demonstrate that impact, then this book is for you too. We hope you enjoy it. We welcome conversation about what we all need to do to keep making a difference to the people and communities we care about.

Sarah Morton and Ailsa Cook
March 2022

1

Why is it so hard to know if you are making a difference?

Do you really know if your organisation, project, programme, service or initiative is making a difference? And are you able to confidently share the story of the difference you're making with funders, commissioners and other stakeholders? **We suspect that if you are reading this book, the answers to these questions might not be as strong as you would like.** You are not alone. This is an issue that has taxed governments, philanthropists, public service organisations big and small and evaluators all over the world for many years.

We engage with teams who strongly believe in the work they do and know implicitly that it does make a difference. However, when they need to report on the difference they're making, they struggle to bring together and evidence a story that paints a realistic picture of their contribution to change.

If you work in public services in the public or third sector and this sounds familiar, then this book is for you.

This chapter explores why it is so hard to know if projects, programmes, partnerships and organisations are making a difference, and what is needed to go on the journey to be able to make evidenced claims that really demonstrate impact.

Specifically, this chapter covers:

- why it is so hard to know the difference you are making;
- the benefits of knowing the difference you are making;
- what you need to go on this journey; and
- our approach to understanding if you are making a difference.

By reading this chapter we hope you will understand why we are writing this book, and what we are going to cover in the rest of the chapters, including an orientation to where you might focus your reading, depending on what you want to know.

Why it is so hard to know the difference you are making

Traditionally, public service systems have been focused on activity and outputs, rather than process and outcomes. This flows into the data and evidence that are captured. There aren't many well-developed and embedded ways of understanding the difference an initiative makes. Indeed, there is often disagreement about what is the right approach. As a result, organisations face different demands for different kinds of data, which makes it hard to commit to any one approach.

Many of us are working in public service systems that are going through a shift in thinking. This is a very welcome shift away from single services to partnerships and alliances; from simple delivery to holistic and people centred. This includes many new ways of working, with more focus on how problems are shifted across a system, and the input of intermediary organisations and boundary spanners, with communications and influencing work taking place alongside service and practice delivery and development. These new ways of working push the boundaries of current evaluative practice.

Evaluating complex, people-based change is inherently hard. It is something that evaluators and academics have been wrestling with for years (Patton, 2011). There have been two main responses to this evaluation challenge. One is to develop elaborate measurement approaches, which can be effective if very well resourced over large sample sizes, but these approaches are not applicable to everyday evaluation for people working in public services and wanting to learn, improve and evaluate on the job. The other response is overly simplistic and focuses on capturing simple numerical data and a case study. This might be adequate for some services; for example, if the work is very static, it might be good enough to persuade others you are doing a good job. But this kind of simple measurement is not enough to really know you're making a difference.

The good news is that we know from our experience of working with more than 130 organisations over the past five years that it *is* possible to know you are making a difference and to share this confidently and clearly with others. The bad news is that there are no magic wands.

If your work focuses on educating, empowering, inspiring, supporting, encouraging or influencing people, then simplistic, quantitative approaches can't tell the story of what difference the work makes, nor *how* it makes that difference.

While the idea of being able to count the impact of work is seductive, the reality is that focusing only on numbers obscures the very aspect of this kind of work that makes it so special – the people.

Equally, understanding how an initiative contributes to change is not something that can be handed over wholesale to an external consultant or evaluator. Drawing on external evaluators can be very helpful in bringing additional expertise and capacity, but handing evaluation over to someone else is only a sticking plaster. It might enable an organisation to tell a good story once, but we would argue that public service organisations need approaches that help them make decisions every day.

The benefits of investing in knowing the difference you are making

In this book we outline an approach to describing and evidencing the difference you are making that builds on everyday practice. We believe that *knowing* you are making a difference is critical to *making* a difference and delivering what is needed to tackle enduring problems. Here are some of the benefits of taking the time to understand the difference being made:

- **Getting funding:** creating a robust and credible plan to illustrate how any work will make a difference, with evidence to support it, will be attractive to funders.

- **Sustaining and scaling up initiatives:** by being able to evidence that new or existing ways of working are making a difference.
- **Making better decisions:** having a clear vision helps to know where to invest and where not to invest. Having real-time data on progress helps to understand where action is needed.
- **Responding to multiple demands for data:** streamlined data systems make it easier to get the granular intelligence needed more quickly.
- **Confident staff:** people want their work to be meaningful. Being able to see the difference it makes helps all staff, but can be particularly important to staff who are removed from direct benefit because they work in information services, as intermediaries or in other non-frontline roles.
- **More influence:** being able to illustrate *whether* an initiative makes a difference is good but showing *how* it makes that difference is key to having influence. That means creating a rich repository of information that can be shared with others to support the spread of practice and to demonstrate to policy makers and funders the effectiveness of the work.
- **Becoming a learning organisation:** considering the difference an initiative makes is the first step to becoming a learning organisation. It provides opportunities for reflection and sharing learning, including about what has and hasn't worked. It helps bring critical thinking to the work being done.
- **Becoming an outcome-focused organisation:** understanding what success looks like becomes a virtuous habit. Setting out a vision for change spreads to other areas of work; for example, thinking about what is important to people, what is needed from meetings and being more focused on what is important about the contribution any work is trying to make.
- **Making the best contribution possible:** together, all of this enables organisations to make the best contribution possible to outcomes with the resources they have available. It helps avoid getting stuck down dead ends and keeps the focus on the changes that matter to improving outcomes.

Our approach will equip organisations and teams to realise these benefits through outcome and impact mapping and tracking. We have seen this many times, and we want people reading this book to benefit by starting on their own journey. We know this works for any initiative where simple numbers can't tell the whole story. Figure 1.1 sets out the types of initiatives we know can benefit.

So, if you are interested in getting to grips with knowing whether an initiative that fits into these descriptions is making a difference, then we invite you to join us on this journey towards getting the understanding, data and evidence you need.

What you need to go on this journey

There is no quick fix to do this work (it wouldn't need a whole book if there were), but there are things that can help on this journey. We set these out in practical ways across the book and in Chapter 10 draw together what it looks like in different organisations and settings. So, to orientate you at the start of this book, and maybe the start of your own journey, we want to mention some of the things that we know people we have worked with needed to make this as smooth as possible.

A strategic approach

We have learnt that understanding the difference any initiative makes is as much a strategic as a practical or even technical task. This requires leadership: to span old and new ways of thinking, and to navigate jargon. Having a clear sense of the difference any initiative wants to make and then assessing progress towards it is a great way of holding onto ownership of what is important to the work, however challenging the external context.

Embedding learning and evaluation into organisational practice

Taking an embedded approach to evaluation – so that learning while doing is in the culture of the work – means that understanding the difference an initiative makes can be more

5

Figure 1.1: Work and organisations where outcome and impact mapping and tracking works

When people are at the heart of change

In work that focuses on educating, empowering, inspiring, supporting, encouraging, or influencing people.

In various sectors

Across all parts of public services — public sector, voluntary sector, NGOs, health, education, social work and care, service providers, intermediaries, partnerships, policy makers, policy-influencing organisations, research initiatives, local and national governments, international bodies and other initiatives.

When navigating complex issues and environments

Including adult care and wellbeing, mental health, children's services, recovery, trauma-informed approaches, food security, ending violence, transforming care, public health, creative approaches, participation and co-production, and COVID recovery.

practically achievable and avoids duplication. Streamlining administrative and evaluative data, embracing reflection for learning and data collection, and creating systems where everyone is involved all help organisations be better informed and more able to tell their story.

It is **vital to engage culture, systems and practice** – we discuss this further below.

Public service improvement as practice

Framing public service reform as a set of practices helps to highlight the processes and systems needed to support these new practices. Social practice theory suggests that this should include what new thinking is needed to work in this way, what competencies and skills people need, and what materials – resources, systems and tools – will help the system change (Shove et al, 2012).

Meanings: ideas and aspirations

The ideas and aspirations of 21st-century public services are very different from what has gone before. This can be considered a new way of thinking, and it requires new competencies and skills to support new ways of working. Through analysing this shift in thinking, it becomes clear what ideas and practices need to be let go of, as well as those that should be embraced.

Figure 1.2 introduces concepts that we will visit many times over the course of the following chapters. Rather than proving what works, the new thinking acknowledges that every context requires continual learning and improving to make sure it keeps working in the context. Shifting accountability to learning rather than performance allows for a culture that can be more in tune with the complex context. Rather than management from the top, and delivering everything the same way everywhere, a governance approach allows services and programmes to be tailored to the context. Leadership is distributed, and leaders are allowed to shape the change needed in their specific settings.

This requires parallel new thinking about the evidence needed for this shift, and the outcomes and impact. We set these out in Chapters 2 and 4.

Figure 1.2: New thinking for public service design, development and delivery

OLD THINKING — NEW THINKING

OLD THINKING	NEW THINKING
Prove what works	Continually improve
Accountability for performance	Accountability for learning
Manage public services	Govern public services
Top-down command and control	Shape and lead complex change

Competencies: skills, knowledge, technique

Although we bring research skills to this work, we don't believe that these are the most important skills and competencies. Rather, everyone needs critical reflection and analysis skills to be able to listen and record what is important and to respond and change what they do based on feedback. Leaders need skills in outcome- and impact-based working, great communication skills to bring people along on the journey and to understand what evidence use looks like. Data and evidence people are essential in this work – not technicians but people who understand evidence to action as a relational process, who can bring together multiple forms of data and can manage data improvement and use projects.

Materials: objects, technologies

There are material factors that help with this work. The most important of these is enough time to make the shift to working in this way. Investment of time will bring benefits further down the line. Better and more flexible information management systems and qualitative and quantitative data collection tools, alongside analysis and reporting tools, are things we really believe in. Finally, sometimes external help in facilitating sessions on outcomes and impact, to enhance capacity to work with data and support the development of new skills and capabilities, is useful.

Our approach to understanding if you are making a difference

We are writing this book because we have been working with these issues separately throughout our careers and together since 2017. We believe that people working in public services need more support to do these difficult tasks, and that they can be better served by robust thinking and innovative tools to do so.

When we met, Ailsa had been pioneering an approach to outcomes. She had spent her career in and out of academia, working with public servants trying to do a better job of delivering services to support people and communities (Cook and Miller, 2012). Sarah had been working in evidence-to-action roles, within and outside the university, and had taken a mid-life PhD, where she had been introduced to contribution analysis. Together, we could see that contribution analysis, complexity thinking, action research, a meaningful orientation to outcomes, and a good understanding of evidence to action was a powerful mix of pragmatic thinking that would really help with the issues people we worked with faced.

Anchored in practice and the practitioners of public services

We brought an 'unconditional positive regard' (Bozarth, 2013) to the people we worked with — those people in the public or third sectors who spend their working lives trying to tackle these complex public problems. We see these as the practitioners of public service.

Rather than creating a distinction between policy makers — as those making policy nationally or locally — and practitioners — as those working directly with people who need support — we think it is helpful to think about the practice of designing, delivering and governing public services, whether in the public or non-government sectors. With this framing, we can start to build the competencies and skills of 21st-century public service

Table 1.1: The practitioners of public service reform

The practitioners of public service reform
Policy makers
Policy and practice influencers and campaigners
Service designers
Knowledge brokers
People with lived experience
Leaders
Managers
Strategists
Innovators
Implementers
People offering support – practitioners and volunteers

practitioners. These would include people delivering, designing, implementing, influencing and innovating in public services as shown in Table 1.1.

We recognise that these practitioners engage in an art of people-based working – a skilled task of supporting, inspiring, educating, empowering and influencing people. We believe that our approach helps make this task more visible and brings this work to life.

Overview of this book

We have written this book because we want to give people the practical and conceptual tools to confidently understand the difference they are making and to continually learn and improve.

The next three chapters give a conceptual grounding to the ideas and methods presented. These are useful if you want to know *why* you do something before you consider *how* to do it, or if you know you will need to make the case for a different way of working.

Chapter 2 explores the importance of understanding 21st-century public service as operating in a complex environment, and the challenges and opportunities that complexity brings to transforming the system.

Chapter 3 considers the data and evidence environments for most organisations working in this space and explores how data cultures influence these. It presents the shift in thinking needed for data and evidence parallel to the shift for public services introduced earlier.

Chapter 4 explains why we think that outcomes and impacts can be useful tools for navigating this complex world and how they can be operationalised in a meaningful way for this work. It presents the shift in thinking required to work more meaningfully with outcomes.

The following five chapters set out a practical approach, based on our experience, to work with these issues. If you just want to get going, then Chapter 5 might be the place to dive into the 'how to do' part of this book.

Chapter 5 delves into the significance of context for any initiative and practical ways of working with contextual factors.

Chapter 6 sets out our approach to outcome and impact mapping to create a framework for evaluation, learning, improvement, data collection and reporting. This chapter is a must-read and is the cornerstone for what follows.

Chapter 7 examines working practically to get the data, evidence and feedback you need, including practical challenges and issues. We share data collection tools and techniques we use in our work.

Chapter 8 takes on the issues of outcome and impact tracking and introduces ways to work with mixed data sets. If you are new to qualitative data analysis, or to bringing together different kinds of data, this will be a particularly useful read.

Chapter 9 looks at reporting, and why outcome- and impact-focused reporting is so powerful. It takes into account different kinds of reporting for different audiences and how to embed a learning, improvement and reporting cycle into this work.

The final two chapters pull together advice about applying the approach to different types of work and some resources that might be helpful.

Chapter 10 thinks about what this looks like in different settings and gives advice for starting out on an outcome evaluation and data improvement journey.

Chapter 11 shares approaches that our clients have found useful and resources that support this way of working. We are delighted to have co-authored this chapter with some of the people we work with, to bring you practical and useful advice.

Try it yourself

Where are you on your journey to knowing the difference your work makes?

- Do you understand the complexity and context of your work and are you able to talk about it to staff, funders and stakeholders? If not, read Chapters 2 and 5.
- Do you know the outcomes and impacts you are seeking – and are these clearly set out for your organisation? If not, read Chapters 3 and 6.
- Do you know if you are capturing the data you need as part of your everyday operations? If not, read Chapters 4 and 7.
- Do you have systems in place for analysing your data, assessing processes and capturing the shared learning from this? If not, read Chapters 4 and 8.
- Do you have a streamlined approach to reporting, visible across the organisation? If not, read Chapter 9.

2

Why complexity thinking can help you understand public services

You are probably reading this book because you care about making things better for people or communities – through providing services, improvement projects and programmes, policy influencing, systems change or practice influencing. What is interesting and what these have in common is that they are not simple change mechanisms – they sit in complex webs of services, programmes, policies and practices, and are not under the control of any one organisation. Instead, change happens through a web of interlinked, overlapping approaches and services.

For initiatives that want to understand the change they make – and make the best change possible – they need to engage with this complexity, with thinking, approaches and tools that embrace and suit the world in which they operate. But working in a way that is compatible with this complexity can be challenging and doesn't always sit well with current ways of doing things.

In this chapter we dig into some of the main issues we have seen people grappling with when trying to do this difficult work. This chapter considers:

- a shift in thinking for complexity-informed approaches;
- working with complex systems;
- people at the heart of complex change;
- evaluating in complexity;
- how our approach helps to work with complexity.

We hope in this chapter you will find familiar ideas and new ones, and it will help orientate your thinking to the challenges of delivering, developing and influencing public services in the 21st century. We want you to feel informed about the importance of complexity for delivering people-based work and have ammunition to argue for complexity-informed ways of monitoring and evaluating for your own change programmes.

A shift in thinking for complexity-informed approaches

Around the world, governments and organisations (for example, the Australian Government, 2019; The Manchester Partnership, 2021) are bringing new thinking to understand the problems that public services are tackling.

The way this is expressed across settings has differences and nuances, but this shift in thinking usually includes the following:

- A recognition that **people's problems are complex and messy** with lots of interdependencies that are unlikely to be solved with single initiatives and programmes.
- An understanding that **people are best placed to know what they need and what action to take**, and that building on an asset-based model rather than a deficit one is more productive and empowering.
- Acknowledgement that service approaches that work alongside people are more effective than those that 'do' things to people, and that the best support **starts with what matters to them**.
- Addressing complex challenges requires **system-wide solutions** and a move away from siloed, service-led approaches and towards working alongside people and communities in partnerships, bringing together all the relevant agencies and making the most of personalisation, partnership and co-production.
- Understanding that tackling complex problems is not just about direct service delivery but also approaches to **governance, leadership, evidence and improvement**.
- Acknowledgement of the need to use evidence well in the current data-rich environment. This means **more emphasis**

on evidence to action and using data intelligently and
in context, and corralling the evidence-generating and use
resources in universities and national agencies.
• There is a need to communicate, influence and convene
systems, and to support system processes such as
partnership working, a focus on learning needs and evidence
to action.

Tackling this new agenda for public services – to make the
best difference possible for people and to understand how that
difference is being made – requires a reorientation of some of the
ways people are used to working. That might include permission
to try new approaches, some of which might not work; using
different and new ways of understanding change that are more
nuanced and less measurement focused; tailoring initiatives to the
very specific context where they occur rather than 'spreading'
the same approaches everywhere; and collaborating across
traditional professional, sectoral and physical boundaries. This
new agenda implies a spirit of cooperation, distributed leadership,
experimentation and evidence use that might be a long way
from business as usual. (For further discussion of these issues,
see: Christie, 2011; Osborne and Strokosch, 2013; Needham
and Mangan, 2016; The Manchester Partnership, 2021.)

For example, a wellbeing service focused on what matters
to people – the personal outcomes that matter to beneficiaries
of the initiative – might be funded as a partnership between a
community organisation and an agency that supports individual
people. It might bring together different professionals, from
social care and social work, health, community development and
local planners. These professionals might spend time thinking
about the specific context for the work and working with
local people to understand what matters to them. They might
work well together to deliver a range of support to people who
are able to articulate that they are more active, happier, more
connected with their communities. They might learn about
partnership working, break down barriers between professionals
and understand better ways of working together. They might try
innovations (such as delivering a walking group for a particular
minority they have been in conversation with) which work,

and those which fail. They can see the difference the work is making but they struggle to show how change for individuals links to changes within the community, or to influence the decision-making structures about how to reorientate other services to be more focused on what matters to people. They are likely to be asked to report on how many individuals are measured as having better wellbeing, but much less likely to be asked to report on wider or more nuanced factors such as happiness, how partnership working is changing delivery and what effect the work is having on the local community. They are extremely unlikely to be asked to show how experimentation led to learning, sometimes failure, but eventually improvement.

Working with complex systems

To make the shift to this new way of doing things, it doesn't make sense to ignore complexity or hope that old ways of working can somehow make do. The importance of taking complexity into account is now widely recognised as essential to understanding change programmes and to evaluating them (CECAN, 2020).

It's good to be clear about what is meant by complexity. Lots of people start explaining complexity by comparing the processes of baking a cake (simple), building a rocket (complicated) and raising a child (complex).

Simple initiatives, such as baking, follow a set of linear instructions, with no particular expertise needed, and the outcome is predictable and replicable, as long as the instructions are followed. For complicated initiatives, expertise is needed and there might be many sets of instructions, but the outcome is specified. In the realm of the complex, however, instructions are no longer suitable; instead, interpretation and navigation are required in a dynamic environment, which highlights the need for data and feedback to be readily available. There can be no specific predictable outcome, but outcomes may be useful to aid navigation, and other unexpected outcomes may emerge.

When initiatives seek to address tenacious social problems that have multiple causes and interlocking factors, they are complex. For example, addressing food insecurity in a local area might include increasing supply of better food, influencing local or

Figure 2.1: Defining complex

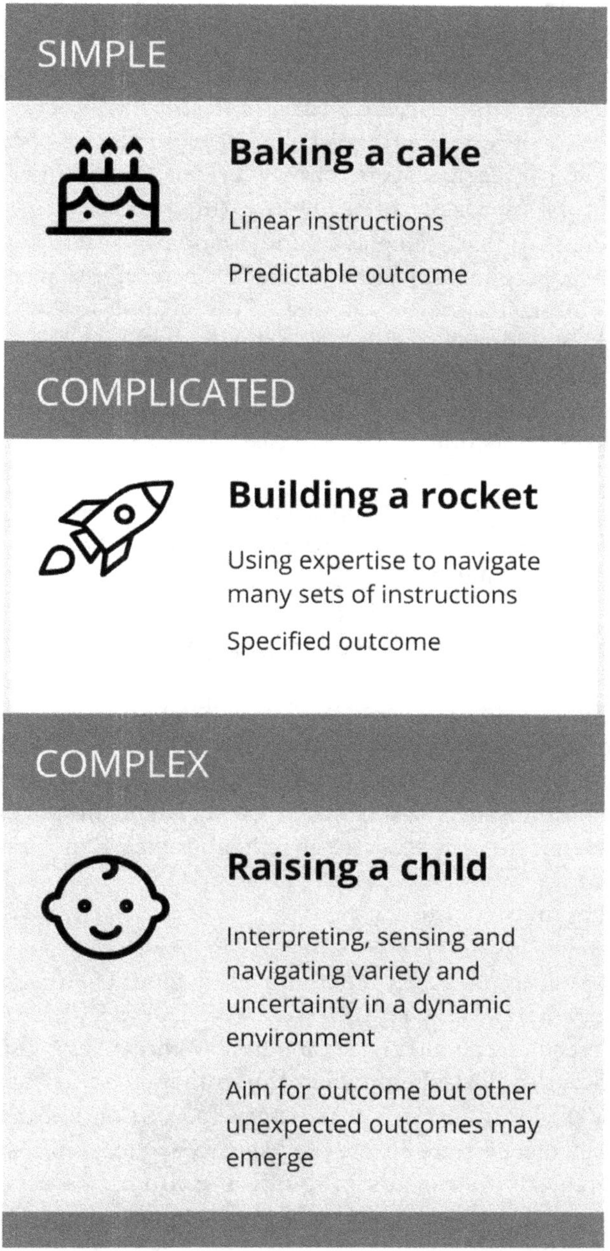

SIMPLE

Baking a cake

Linear instructions

Predictable outcome

COMPLICATED

Building a rocket

Using expertise to navigate many sets of instructions

Specified outcome

COMPLEX

Raising a child

Interpreting, sensing and navigating variety and uncertainty in a dynamic environment

Aim for outcome but other unexpected outcomes may emerge

wider policies about what is available, equipping people with the skills they need, bringing people together to celebrate food culture. This would require partnership working across agencies, and it would be easier to make a difference together than it would for any one of these alone.

What are the implications of seeing these problems as complex, and how should managers, change makers, practitioners and evaluators approach them? Doing this well requires new approaches to management, to understanding what is working and to helping initiatives stay on track. To recognise what that means in practical terms, the rest of this chapter looks further into the components of complex systems and how they affect managing, navigating and evaluating public service initiatives.

First, it can be useful to understand some of the core components of complex systems (see Table 2.1).

Working well with the interlocking factors defined in Table 2.1 requires careful thinking and orientation. We think that there are good ways of navigating and managing in these complex environments.

Doing the right thing, not the same thing every time

Making the shift to this new way of working means sensing and interpreting in the specific context for the work in hand. We often refer to this as 'doing the right thing' as opposed to doing the same thing over and over. Doing the right thing to make a difference for people is rarely straightforward and involves accepting a few truths.

Doing the right thing means:

- Doing it appropriately differently every time. There is no one intervention that will work for everyone, everywhere.
- Approaching people's and communities' challenges holistically and doing all of the different things they need to move on in their lives. Services or initiatives focused on one specific aspect of a person's life are less likely to be successful. Weight Watchers understands this, offering food, classes, food-tracking techniques, information and support, which together make the difference.

Table 2.1: Components of complex systems

Core component of complex systems	Implications
Many interactions between people and place	This leads to unpredictable outcomes and patterns. Just because something is effective in one place or at a specific time doesn't mean it will be the same next time. People are different in every place. It can be useful to think of any initiative as embedded in the system, rather than separate to it, and look for these interactions between people and place as they happen.
Interventions, programmes and approaches affect one another	No organisation or initiative is operating in a vacuum. This means consideration of how external services, policies and structures affect any work is important. Where are the synergies and challenges? What needs to be in place to ensure success, and what might cut across it? What can be done to steer the system towards the outcomes that matter?
Previous policies, ways of working, structures and processes continue to affect the system	Past policies, such as de-industrialisation, housing programmes and childcare policies, are still influencing what is happening now. It can be hard to change direction if there has been a strong push for a particular approach and that has been embedded in the system. Sometimes it takes huge disruptions, like the COVID-19 pandemic, to shift to different ways of working. Acknowledging and looking out for these path dependencies can help navigate them.
Feedback loops – information and knowledge can have large system effects	Evaluation and direct data are the main feedback loops for learning and improvement, but they're not the only ones. Often, there are stories about people and place, and success and failure, that affect how people think and act. It's good to try to be aware of these and the effect they have on what's being done now. System influencers also create stories and share case studies to exemplify and highlight the change they want to work towards.

- Understanding the situation from the perspective of the people you're working with to make the change. Whether they're people using services, policy makers or the general public, it's their definition of success or failure that is important.
- Not just rolling out what was done last time, but carefully designing an initiative for the outcomes or impacts that matter, in the context and for the people involved.

Doing the right thing means that initiatives are much more likely to make the difference they want to, but it does sometimes involve letting go of current practices and embracing new ones. For example, we know that projects and programmes can rarely be delivered perfectly to time, as planned and following evidence-based protocols. Instead, planning and delivery need to be informed by evidence and constantly sense-making in a complex environment, as we discuss in more detail in Chapter 3. It means making a shift from focusing on internal organisation dynamics, functioning and activities to the relationship to the people and communities they hope to benefit or influence. This involves thinking through what success looks like for the people at the heart of change, what they need to get there and how they can be best engaged. These questions frame what is needed before any initiative can fully focus on the components of delivery.

It is not what we do, but how we do it that makes a difference. Relationships are integral to this. We would go as far as to say that it's not possible to deliver public services without a focus on relationships. Many people recognise this from personal experience – the difference, for example, between talking to a GP who greets you warmly, asks how you are doing and really listens, versus one who seems too busy and distant to care. They're both ten-minute appointments, but one leaves you empowered and ready to tackle the issue and the other confused and unsure.

This way of working opens enormous new possibilities and opportunities, especially for staff delivering initiatives. There's no drudgery when people are constantly focused on doing the right thing and knowing they are making the best difference they can. Everyone's creativity and contribution are valued. This has been called 'good relational practice' and is a tenet of what Needham and Mangan (2016) describe as a core competency of the 21st-century public servant.

Ways of managing in complexity

Doing the right thing every time is key in shifting towards a complexity-informed and effective public service design, delivery or influencing model. For those charged with managing, designing and delivering these new ways of working, there are aspects of managing in complex systems that are helpful to consider:

- **Context sensitivity:** Being sensitive to the specific context for an initiative, and adapting and embedding initiatives appropriately differently every time. It's not possible to just replicate or make prescriptions about 'what works'. Gaining a clear understanding of the local system and what that means for appropriate interventions is crucial. In Chapter 5, we explain ways of working well, with context and tools that can help.
- **Embed learning and reflection:** Having the right information and feedback as approaches are developed and rolled out is key. This helps with testing assumptions, learning, adapting as things change and checking progress. Learning fast when things aren't working, without blame or fear of failure, allows for quick adaptation and improvement.
- **Working together:** Partnership is essential for complex interventions as initiatives and organisations interact. This includes being clear about the specific contribution of different partners to the same issue or problem, as well as what needs to be in place to be successful.
- **Put relationships front and centre:** People are key when working with complex issues – whether at the front line or in designing policies and interventions. Concentrating on people and relationships, highlighting their importance and purposely fostering them is more effective than a technocratic approach.
- **Many perspectives:** It's easier to understand and work with a system if many perspectives are included that reflect the ways the system plays out for different people.
- **Thinking at levels:** Complex systems are often thought of as operating at macro, meso and micro levels – thinking through any strategies at each of these levels and who is important at each one can be helpful.
- **Data gathering and use strategies:** Evidence and data need to be used flexibly and responsively to explore what works, how, when, where and for whom. This is discussed in more detail in the next section.

Navigating through complexity

Navigating through complexity, taking on board the issues described and trying to ensure the work reflects the complexity without becoming overwhelmed by it, can be challenging. It might help to think of this as a complex–simple scale (Figure 2.2).

Figure 2.2 shows that approaches can become too simplistic – not representing the complexity of the work in hand – and also too complex, in their approaches to mapping, designing and supporting. Ideally, work needs to be both simple enough and complex enough.

It would be nice if there were a perfect place on this scale that could be reached – complex enough to represent the complex world of the work being done, but simple enough to offer insight into what is happening. Perhaps a more realistic view is that there is constant recalibration within the shaded zone as new information comes in, new approaches are tried and understanding is built. Complexity-informed leaders and change makers constantly sense make along this scale as they navigate the landscape for their work.

The rest of this chapter considers the people who are key in getting to this middle space where complexity is taken into account, but not overwhelmingly so, and what all of this means for evaluation.

Figure 2.2: Designing work on the complex–simple scale

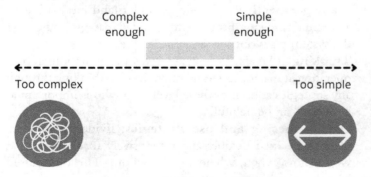

People at the heart of complex change

Embracing complexity and working with change that has people at its core means that those people need to be in sharp focus. People need to be included to frame and understand change, to understand what is significant about context, to plan engagement well and to understand the system. This section sets out some helpful ways of bringing focus to the people that matter.

People experience the system in different ways

As we've discussed, it can be hard to see what is going on in a fast-changing system influenced internally and externally by many unpredictable factors. Managers or implementers make assumptions (based on previous knowledge and experience) when planning initiatives. These assumptions might be about what practice or policy looks like, how services work, or what a needs assessment is telling them. In order to get a 360 degree view of a system, it is really helpful to include and embrace the people who are focal to any initiative. In our work, we often get those managers and implementers, along with front-line staff, service user representatives, funders, partners and wider stakeholders, in the room to think about the context in which an initiative operates, and how it will work. We say more about what this looks like practically in Chapters 5 and 6.

It is easy to identify beneficiaries and targets of services, strategies or programmes, but who else is central to success? This will include partner organisations, other services or provisions the initiative needs to have in place (for example a physical health programme may rely on mental health support being available elsewhere), the staff groups and organisations central to delivery, and the funders and authorisers (see Chapter 5).

Co-production and participatory approaches

Given the role that people and relationships play in the system, and the effect that including them has on the success or otherwise of initiatives, it is unsurprising that co-production and participation are common building blocks of the vision for public services for the 21st century. While both co-production and participation are poorly defined terms that mean different things to different people, evidence suggests that embracing these models does help sharpen the effectiveness of services. We advocate for including people in planning, learning, reflecting and reporting on initiatives, and co-production and participation models offer a particular way of building long-term relationships with people who will help improve and navigate the system.

The 'who' in data and feedback

Another way to ensure people are at the heart of how change is planned for, refined and understood is to think carefully about who matters in data collection. This is one of the obvious places where numbers can't tell the story of what is important in a change programme. Finding out and recording what people think, how they have been involved, what they have learned and gained, and what they are doing differently in their own words can be powerful, and an excellent resource for learning, sensing and improving. Finding this out from service beneficiaries is a beneficial thing to do. We encourage feedback from partners, staff members, people delivering initiatives, policy makers and anyone else integral to the success of the endeavour. We explore this further below and offer practical ways of carrying it out in Chapter 7.

Leadership for complex work

Leadership might look quite different with this way of working. Rather than top-down hierarchical approaches, leaders need to enable everyone to work in a complexity-informed way, delivering in the manner that is appropriate to the context and the people they're dealing with. When trying new things, there will be some that don't work, and so leaders are needed who are brave enough to own the learning from failure and who won't be penalised for failure by the organisations they work in. They'll need to keep going when things are tough and to own the emotional component of complex change.

Relationships of all kinds are at the heart of making a difference, so a deliberate focus on them is an obvious but powerful tool to making a difference and to demonstrating change.

Evaluating in complexity

It's clear that evaluating and understanding the difference any initiative is making is hard. Navigating the multiple factors influencing change, understanding complexity but not being overwhelmed by it, focusing on the main relationships and embracing the specific challenges of the setting are the framing factors that create these difficulties.

As we set out in the introduction, we work – day in and out – with some amazing pioneering organisations who are taking on this challenge because they really care about the difference they want to see in the world and want to make the best difference they can. We believe we have developed tools and approaches, alongside robust concepts, that make this evaluation work not only doable but also enjoyable and rewarding.

The central concept of 'contribution'

One of the ways that evaluators address the challenges of complex systems is to use contribution analysis. This was initially set out by John Mayne (2008) and is one of the cornerstones of our approach.

What is so powerful about contribution analysis is that it provides both the concept and the tools to address some of the challenges. The first part of this is separating the concepts of attribution and contribution. When complex systems are at play, then there is no direct cause and effect. The concept of attribution – direct cause and effect – works well for drugs: you have a headache, you take a tablet, the tablet causes your headache to go away. This model is essential for drugs, health devices and other settings where the system is closed and other factors are predictable, but not for public services where the system is open, complex and fast moving. As Figure 2.3 shows, external influences are unpredictable and change quickly. (The

Figure 2.3: Understanding cause and effect: contribution vs attribution

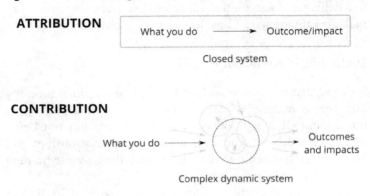

COVID-19 pandemic is a great example of this.) There are so many influences on high-level outcomes that no one initiative can cause them on their own. The term 'contribution', and the thinking that it evokes, is the foundation for applying contribution analysis and working more meaningfully with the outcomes that matter to any initiative.

Making a difference to people and communities is difficult and complex public sector work. Viewing it with a contribution lens helps understand that multiple contributions will be needed across the system to tackle a single problem. For example, to address obesity in a specific geographical place, there is a need for individual support on food and exercise, but without addressing food availability and affordability, education for children and adults, and the food industry's role, it is unlikely to have a sustained effect. Increasingly, governments acknowledge the need for this whole systems approach in which multiple initiatives each make their contribution to the issue – for example, that of the UK Government (Public Health England, 2019).

Contribution analysis

Contribution analysis is a pragmatic approach to working within this complex systems lens to understand the difference that any initiative, policy, programme or project makes. It explores how the actions of an initiative contribute to making a difference, alongside other factors.

At its core are six steps that we have adapted and used with many teams over the last 15 years. The six steps at the heart of this approach are:

1. Understand the problem you seek to address and the system in which it sits.
2. Develop a 'theory of change': how projects or programmes aim to create change.
3. Assemble and use existing data and evidence (like routinely collected data).
4. Assess any gaps in the evidence of success.
5. Seek out additional evidence.
6. Create a contribution story.

Throughout the rest of this book, we are going to present how we have built on this way of working by undertaking context analysis; developing a theory of change – an outcome or impact map; tracking progress across that map using a mixed and pragmatic approach to data and evidence; assessing progress and gaps in evidence; and telling the story to different audiences. You can see these steps reflected in the content of Chapters 5 to 9.

Appropriately different evaluation every time

Setting out how a specific initiative will work towards outcomes and impacts and doing that in a way that is informed by the contextual factors that influence it – doing the right thing appropriately differently – means that evaluation also needs to be done appropriately differently for each initiative. That means defining its own outcomes and impacts and deciding on appropriate data. Evaluation in these complex settings must be bespoke to the work in hand. It needs to build on a strong understanding of how the work *can* make a difference in this particular setting and use that as the foundation for determining whether it does make that difference.

How our approach helps to work with complexity

Despite the challenges illustrated, we believe there are good practical ways of working with complexity to develop initiatives, policies and practices that can address 21st-century problems. Indeed, we think that practitioners – of public services design, policy, influence and delivery – must work with these issues to move forward with the biggest and most pressing challenges of our time.

Building blocks of our complexity-informed approach

The outcome- and impact-tracking approach we communicate in this book builds on contribution analysis but brings in other approaches and principles that we have developed and refined over many years of supporting organisations to understand the difference they make.

Complexity-informed: embracing and understanding complexity, as described in this chapter.
Evidence to action: seeing evidence use as relational and dynamic, as expressed in Chapter 3.
Meaningful approach to outcomes and impacts: using these approaches to help create vision and direction, and avoiding crass and simple measures, as discussed in Chapter 4.
The right tools: our innovative and flexible software, OutNav, was built to support and embed this way of working, and we will briefly explain in each chapter how it does this.

Bringing these together into a practical approach is laid out in the rest of this book.

Try it yourself

After reading this chapter you might want to take some time to think, and discuss with colleagues, how complexity-informed your work is, and how you might bring some of the concepts from here into the way you frame and drive your work, as well as understand your impact.

Questions for exploring the complexity of your work

Do you regularly discuss and analyse the context for the work? What do you do with this information? How do you adapt if external changes affect what you are doing?

Do you focus on people and use co-production or other collaborative approaches? Are you thorough about who is included in any feedback mechanisms you use?

What is your appetite for innovation, experimentation and failure? What happens when things go wrong? Are these seen as learning opportunities or do people have to take the blame?

Have you tried thinking about the system you work in through the levels of micro (what goes on between people in a day-to-day way), meso (the organisational factors and interorganisational issues) and macro (the wider problem and setting, policy initiatives and politics)? What insights does thinking on these different levels give you?

These concepts are developed throughout the book, where you can find more help and guidance.

3

What data and evidence do you need to see what difference you are making?

In this chapter we are going to explore what data, evidence and feedback practices are helpful or unhelpful for knowing whether you are making a difference. Initially, we are going to dig into some of the cultures and practices that we know get in the way of having the feedback you need to understand change.

We will talk about the data and evidence that is best suited to understanding complex change. We will draw on our experience of working in different settings to explore data cultures that exist in all organisations. We will think about how these data cultures can help or hinder initiatives to do the right thing, and know they are doing the right thing. We will give some examples and highlight ways of applying this thinking to any specific work, especially making the case for using mixed data that includes qualitative data. We will then lay out what it means to go on a data improvement journey and offer some practical ways of thinking about the data and evidence needs in any specific setting.

In this chapter we set out:

- good data and evidence for complex change;
- data cultures and how they affect organisations and initiatives;
- making the case for qualitative data;
- getting started on a data improvement journey.

If data, evidence and feedback is something that excites and interests you (and it is definitely something that excites and interests us!), then you will enjoy reading the arguments and issues we take from this chapter forward into Chapter 7, where we look in more detail at practical ways to start on a data and evidence improvement journey. We hope that this chapter will arm you with the arguments you need to make the case for the approaches to data, evidence and feedback that can help you understand if you are making a difference.

What is included when we talk about data, evidence and feedback?

We talk in this chapter, and elsewhere in the book, about data, evidence and feedback. We want to encompass all the ways that any organisation uses information about what it does to understand what difference it makes. For most organisations, this is a complicated mix of different kinds of more or less formally collected data that might be very disorganised across different areas of work, or patchy (well organised in some parts but less so in others). We believe that most organisations need to go on a data improvement journey to get to a point where they have the data they need to understand what difference they are making. When we use the term 'data', or 'data, evidence and feedback', we mean all of the information that is relevant to your organisation's change programmes. This includes:

Data: any quantitative, numerical or qualitative information collected about what you are doing and what difference it makes. This could be data gathered through day-to-day work and data captured specifically for evaluation purposes.
Feedback: any formal or informally collected feedback that you are using (or even just informally discussing) to understand what is going on. This can include what people say directly to you about your work, or data gathered through feedback forms or surveys.
Formal evidence: more formal and processed information, such as evaluation reports (yours or from other similar work) and research evidence – systematic reviews, research that relates to the themes of your work, and so on. 'Evidence' can also be used informally as a term to refer to all of the above.

Evidence from practice: the informally generated evidence teams get from reflecting systematically on practice; this could be through reflective practice sessions, team meetings, action learning groups, reflective logs. This form of evidence is generally underutilised by organisations, but easy to gather.

Good data and evidence for complex change

The argument we have set out so far – that people in public services need to embrace a vision fit for the 21st century that recognises the complexity of the issues people face, tailors responses to place and people, and focuses on doing the right thing every time – raises some big questions for data, evidence and feedback. Lots of organisations are working though the shift from top-down hierarchical approaches focused on scrutiny, accountability, control and judgement to people-centred, responsive, multilayered ones focused on what's needed for people and communities. But data, evidence and feedback practices and approaches have a hard time trying to keep up! Many are not suited to understanding the effectiveness of programmes, policies and interventions operating in complex environments.

Dominant approaches to public service management and ensuring good value, over decades, have required organisations to generate swathes of data in exchange for funding or permission to do their work. Internationally, these approaches to planning, delivering and managing the performance of public services are underpinned by data and evidence systems that seek to reduce the complexity of the delivery and outcomes of public services into convenient measures, indicators and targets.

As a result, often public service organisations are laden with approaches to data and evidence that are simplistic and reductionist in nature. These are based on an approach to understanding the world that seeks to split it into measurable components at different levels. This works really well for things important to public services that can be reduced to meaningful, measured units; for example, age and number of people who have received a vaccination or have been infected with a disease. Gathering this data and doing so well is critical to effective delivery. The problems come when public service organisations try to, or are expected to, use simple measures to understand complex issues, such as whether an initiative is making a difference.

When planning your approach to use of data and information, it is important to remember that simple measures:

- don't take account of what goes on between people, the relationships at the heart of change;
- ignore or minimise what is going on in the wider context, implying that each intervention is delivered separately, when this is never the case (as well as the role of other services and interventions, wider conditions such as housing, employment, family issues and similar contextual factors have a huge impact on what things are like for people and communities);
- imply that change is simpler than it is, by focusing on isolated factors or components. In fact, there are many complex and interlinked components of how change happens. Measurement needs to embrace and work with that complexity.

The sort of simple measures that are often used to understand change, but are not well suited on their own to complex change, include things such as setting a baseline to measure change against, or standardised scales for health and wellbeing. These might be useful as one component of tracking the difference being made, but on their own will probably mask what is really important. They don't show the quality of relationships at the heart of change, they try to standardise things that are not really measurable (for example confidence) and they don't take account of the impact of wider factors beyond the initiative. A focus on simple measurement of 'results' (often high-level outcomes) masks what it takes to achieve the result, and at worst can lead to gaming the system (for instance, by offering services to those most likely to help reach the measure).

So, the first part of developing a data, evidence and feedback system that will work for any initiative aiming for change in a complex system is to treat simple measurement with caution. There might be aspects that are helpful (usually alongside more qualitative data), or that are required by a funder or stakeholder, but it is always useful to be aware of any limitations, and supplement with data and feedback better suited to the complex setting.

Let's measure what matters

Another problem with taking an oversimplistic view of data is that we focus on what can be measured, rather than what is most important. That's not surprising given that people often want things to be simpler than they are! It would be amazing if the complex world of public service design, policy, management and delivery could be neatly boxed up and counted, but it can't.

As sociologist Cameron (1969) said, 'Not everything that can be counted counts, and not everything that counts can be counted.' Often, public service systems are driven by focusing on the easily measurable things, whether or not these are what matter to people and communities. One of the sectors in which this is most visible is education, where exam results – the most measurable part of the system – are the basis of league tables and funding at the expense of all else. These kinds of measure-driven systems underemphasise the context in which schools operate, the challenges and opportunities presented by the families that attend, as well as what matters to children and their families – things like creativity, belonging, relationships, community service, happiness or wellbeing.

So, when public services are trying to change their focus to the transformation we described earlier, what kinds of measurement are more appropriate?

We believe that it is vital to take a tailored approach to data for public services that always includes qualitative data, alongside a proportionate approach to quantitative data scrutinised to be suitable for the specific work and setting.

This requires a shift in thinking towards a different approach to data, evidence and feedback – one that embraces learning and doing the right thing (see Figure 3.1).

Figure 3.1: New thinking for complexity-informed data and evidence

OLD THINKING		NEW THINKING
What causes change	→	What contributes to change
Evidence-based	→	Evidence-informed
Define measures and indicators	→	Assess data to understand progress
What works	→	How, why and where things work
Count things	→	Bring together numbers, reflections and stories
Validity, reliability	→	Useability
Evaluation follows budget	→	Evaluation focuses on innovation and what we don't already know
Before and after measurement	→	Reflections on progress and change
External evaluation for scrutiny	→	Embedded and transparent self-evaluation
Navigating and reporting on externally defined measures	→	Measures defined for setting and reflected on for learning
Define measures and indicators	→	Collective learning

This book focuses on what is needed in an everyday way to understand what difference public services contribute to, and to embed learning cultures into design, influence and delivery. This means practical approaches to the right data, at the right scale for understanding the specific change at hand. When thinking about any type of data or feedback – collection, analysis and use – the important consideration is what it is being collected and used for. The questions that need to be asked should drive any data collection, along with the capacity to use the data collected. We shall explore this in Chapters 5 and 6. We often hear clients say it is difficult to make the case for taking this more nuanced approach to data, evidence and feedback in their setting. That is why it is so important to address the issue of data cultures.

Data cultures and how they affect organisations and initiatives

Data cultures, like other kinds of culture, are invisible systems of beliefs and practices that underpin what is valued and what is important in any organisation. According to Schein (1985), culture is a set of taken-for-granted assumptions that operate at three different levels: artefacts, the things you can feel and observe about a new culture; values, what people say about the culture; and underlying assumptions, the unconscious taken-for-granted beliefs, habits and feelings. Applying these concepts to the way data is understood, collected and used within an organisation can be a helpful starting point to getting the approach needed to shift to the new paradigm.

What we have observed in our work is that there are sector differences in the basis of these data cultures. In health settings, there is usually a traditional hierarchy of evidence that values systematic reviews and randomised control trials over people's experience (Davies and Nutley, 2000). Of course, that is entirely appropriate for testing the effectiveness of medical interventions focused on the physical world, such as drugs, procedures and devices. However, this culture permeates programmes and approaches that are much less suited to reductionism. People working in services which are not orientated around empirically measurable treatment outcomes, for example public or community health approaches, often find themselves struggling to make the case for the use of more fitting and diverse means of evidencing their work. This traditional data culture can also rub off on other parts of the system, for example the extent to which non-reductionist research is funded.

At the other end of the spectrum, some data cultures value the lived experience of people above all else. They are orientated around ensuring that this lived experience is reflected in everything they do. These kinds of data cultures often prefer informal ways of gathering feedback to formal ones and embrace creativity and inclusion at the core of their feedback systems. These kinds of data cultures can be empowering and innovative, but they can also undervalue more formal ways of understanding the difference they make, struggle when there is disagreement between people about what is important, and don't always include a way of balancing different views.

Most organisations exist somewhere between the traditional reductionist culture and a highly informal one. When trying to understand the core assumptions, values and artefacts of the data culture of your organisation, it can be helpful to consider:

- Is there a dominant paradigm that values certain kinds of data over others?
- Are there data collection systems in place? What kinds of data do they focus on?
- Are there any data requirements as a result of demands from the core, funders or government? What kind of data do these require?
- What resources are allocated to collecting and using data?
- Whose job is it to collect, store and analyse data? What does this say about data for accountability or learning?

The answers to those questions will help to orientate an organisation's data beliefs and values. It's also interesting to consider if there are recent changes to how any organisation approaches questions of data, evidence and feedback. Whatever the current practice, there will be a legacy from the way data has been collected and used in the past. It can take a long time for organisations to change their orientation to data and feedback collection, analysis and use. Change takes time and doesn't happen for everyone or every part of the organisation at the same time.

Making the case for qualitative data

We believe that qualitative data must be included to understand if you are making a difference for complex people-based work. Ways of approaching qualitative data collection and analysis are discussed later in this book, but what we want to address here is the need for this thesedata and how to make the case for qualitative data in a system that more highly values quantitative data. It's first worth understanding some of the differences between these two data types, and what they are more useful for (see Table 3.1).

The extent to which an organisation leans to one or other side of Table 3.1 also says a lot about the data culture. Those leaning towards quantitative approaches might see qualitative data as 'anecdotal' and undervalue how robust it can be. Those focusing only on qualitative data might be missing patterns that

Table 3.1: Comparing purpose and uses of qualitative and quantitative data

Qualitative	Quantitative
Understanding meaning	Measuring
For exploring issues and meanings	For testing hypotheses
Limited generalisability	Potentially generalisable
Focus on reflexivity to build robustness	Focus on validity and reliability
Participant seen as the expert	Researcher seen as the expert
Reflects individual difference	Doesn't seek to understand individual difference

would become apparent with more quantitative approaches. For many organisations, where qualitative data is undervalued, there are often strongly held beliefs about qualitative data that are not helpful. We have often observed the myths shown in Figure 3.2 permeating the data cultures of organisations, and have given the following advice to help move on from these views.

Figure 3.2: Qualitative data myths and busts

MYTHS ABOUT QUALITATIVE DATA   **MYTH BUSTERS**

It is anecdotal and isn't robust enough to help understand what people think. Not enough people are included.

Collected and analysed in a systematic way, qualitative data is robust. Researchers talk about a 'saturation point' (Saunders et al, 2018) when you don't hear any new viewpoints — usually after examining data from 30 to 40 people.

People can use qualitative data to 'spin' a good story about how well they are doing.

Any data has to be interpreted, including quantitative data, and this can be done well or badly (Huff and Geis, 1954). What is important is to show how it has been interpreted so that someone else can understand the judgements that have been made. Making this process as transparent as possible is what makes any claims more robust — regardless of the data type.

It is difficult to handle and know what to do with lots of qualitative data.

There are systematic approaches to handling qualitative data — see Chapter 7.

Capturing evidence from practice – the power of reflection

Many organisations focus their data-gathering efforts on what other people think and want to know about their work, rather than on what they learn through their day-to-day practice. By 'practice', we don't just mean service delivery, but leadership, policy making, governance, strategy, communication, and so on. When working in a complex system, every person in an organisation or team is constantly sensing and adjusting what they do, making hundreds of small decisions in a day that have a bearing on the difference an initiative makes. As we highlighted in Chapter 2, embracing the individual contributions of every staff member, the relationships they build and their judgements in context is essential to working effectively with complexity. Capturing evidence in relation to these aspects of practice is critical to knowing if an initiative is making a difference and to staying focused on making the best difference possible. It has wider benefits too – to really understanding how the work makes a difference, what is getting in the way and what are the strategies that individuals and teams are using to overcome these challenges: all great learning about the work and the complex system in which it sits.

In our experience, the easiest way to capture this valuable evidence is to embed systematic approaches into reflecting on practice and to implement those reflections into day-to-day work in a structured way. These structured recordings can then be analysed and used as evidence. Some examples of how organisations we work with have done this in practice are shared in Chapter 7.

What is happening when people 'use' data?

Finally, it is important to think about what is happening when people 'use' data. Working with data, evidence and feedback is often presented and thought about as a technical-rational process. That's what fits with the reductionist paradigm of separating the world into parts in order to better understand them. But people don't use data in this way – **people interact with knowledge from their own perspective, experience**

and context (Morton, 2015). If we pretend that the people and relationships are unimportant, then we are ignoring the core of the change process. In fact, people have many influences on whether they act on evidence – one of the most important being what their colleagues say and think (Gabbay and Le May, 2004).

So, if people and their perspectives, feelings, passions and needs are at the heart of the data-use process in any organisation, then it's important to work with that and build in people-centred evidence-to-action approaches that support that process. These might be things such as learning cycles and reflective practice – including reflecting on impact and embedding data discussions in team and partnership meetings. It means allowing time and space for data use to be part of delivery, whatever the setting. It means working to become a learning organisation (Garvin, 1993) – which has wider benefits in supporting organisational effectiveness.

Getting started on a data improvement journey

Careful thinking and planning are needed to embrace the challenges of data in this complex work, to start to understand the data culture of any organisation, and to have the data, evidence and feedback needed to understand if an initiative is making a difference. We would describe this work as a data improvement journey. It won't happen instantly, and it'll take time and effort.

When resources are scarce – as they usually are in public service organisations – it's key to focus data collection and use on what is most important. This means that data practices start with a foundation of what is already known. If there is an approach that has been tried and tested for many years, then a light-touch approach to monitoring is sufficient. If some areas of the work have been subjected to rigorous research, then they don't need as much attention.

For example, there is a strong evidence base that giving the poorest children breakfast improves their performance at school (Crawford et al, 2016). If an organisation is running a breakfast club, it doesn't need to be monitoring the performance of the pupils who attend – rather, it can focus efforts on ensuring that the poorest pupils attend consistently, that they are the ones who need support, and that the food is healthy and being eaten. Focusing a limited resource on engaging the families who will benefit most, and understanding that these are the right families, is much more important.

Assembling the existing data (whether administrative, formal, organisational or other) is an important first step on a data improvement journey. This allows organisations to focus their efforts on where there are gaps in data, evidence and feedback, and how to fill those gaps.

If all of this sounds overwhelming, then our advice is just to get started somewhere. It would be great to be able to shake down any organisation's data challenges and quickly have everything in the right place but, unfortunately, it's just not like that.

In Chapter 7, we share practical tools to support the journey. Here, our message is that you can take some simple steps now to make a start, and that once you get going, big changes can begin to happen.

Try it yourself

Here are four things you can do now to get going on your data improvement journey:

1. **Review your recording practices.** Organisations spend a lot of time capturing data and it is always worthwhile making sure that data helps you make better decisions. Pick one aspect of your practice you really care about and then review your recording around this. Do you capture the data you need? How consistent is your recording? Can you do anything with this data and if not, what would you need to change to extract meaningful insights?

2. **Stop gathering data you haven't got the capacity to use.** Gathering data, evidence and feedback with a sense of purpose and a plan for how it will be used and who will be involved, and then carrying out that plan, is powerful. You will get some learning about your work, and your data culture and system, that will help frame your improvement journey.

3. **Use qualitative data.** If you aren't already doing this, then just get started – there are more ideas about how to do this in Chapter 7.
4. **Systematise reflections.** Reflecting on progress or practice is good for learning and improvement, but if you systematise these reflections by capturing them carefully, they can add insightful data to help you understand change. Build reflective questions into your team meetings. If you ask these questions of everyone in the same way, you'll generate robust evidence from practice.

4

Owning your initiative's outcomes and impacts

Being clear about the difference an initiative wants to make and the outcomes or the impacts of the work is the first step in knowing whether it is making a difference. Taking the time to really understand how the work contributes to intended outcomes or impacts brings other benefits too. Getting a clear sense of what matters and the change the work is seeking to make in the world is vital when navigating a complex environment. Having a clear vision for where the work is heading acts as a beacon, providing a firm direction whatever changes around it.

Internationally, public services are dripping with references to outcomes, impacts, outputs, goals and results. Many of the organisations we work with around the world are in a situation where they need to report to or align with multiple outcome frameworks and indicators, sometimes for the same work. This can result in organisations feeling caught in a tangle of outcomes, expected to respond and adapt to the range of approaches taken by their funders, commissioners, policy leads and regulators. Being able to navigate around this complex outcomes and impacts landscape is becoming a key competency for anyone leading public services where they are expected to work towards, report on or be evaluated against outcomes or impacts. This is what we call 'owning your outcomes or impacts'.

If this picture sounds familiar, then this chapter is for you. Over the coming pages we will provide some accessible ways to understand and operationalise outcomes and impacts in your work and unpack some of the contradictions surrounding the use of outcomes and impacts within wider policy and funding systems. In this chapter we will discuss:

- navigating the landscape of outcomes and impacts;
- an introduction to outcome thinking;
- a new way of working with outcomes;
- owning your outcomes and impacts: what this means in practice.

While this chapter can't remove the complexity of your outcomes and impacts landscape, we hope it will give you a vision for what it means to own this and to make you feel more comfortable with what it means for your work. Chapters 5 and 6 provide some practical approaches to help you realise this.

A note on language

Across the world and across sectors, language used to talk about the difference work makes includes:

- outcomes
- impacts
- results
- goals

While there are academics and evaluators who would argue that these terms are distinct, in practice, we find that these terms are generally used in the same ways, and which terms are used is more about sectoral preferences than meaning. For example, *impact* is most commonly used within international development, research and social enterprise; *goals* is used in the Sustainable Development Goals, but also in rehabilitative settings; *results* is used in local government in some geographies and by some philanthropic funders.

Within the Scottish context and elsewhere, *outcomes* is the term used most often and what we will mostly use in this book. What you use is entirely up to you!

Navigating the landscape of outcomes and impacts

All over the world, policy makers, regulators and funders are moving towards outcome-, impact- or results-based approaches that shape the way they prioritise their efforts and resources, and fund, commission, monitor and assure the quality of that work. The benefits or otherwise of this turn towards outcomes and impacts has been widely discussed by academics and others. (If this interests you, see Cook (2017) and the Human Learning Systems website, which gives a good overview of debates.) Generally speaking, the shift towards outcomes comes from a desire to focus public services and spending on important societal challenges and on what matters to people. But it can also be very confusing when multiple outcome- or impact-based approaches are overlaid from international, national, local and specific funders' policies.

Any interaction with outcome-based approaches will be different depending on the sector and context, but usually one or more of the following reasons will drive the shift to this kind of approach.

Drivers of outcome- or impact-based approaches

1. To demonstrate alignment of initiatives with policy or funder outcomes frameworks, for example the Sustainable Development Goals or national or local government outcome frameworks like the ones in Scotland and Wales.
2. To be accountable to policy or funder outcomes; accountability requirements often come along with predefined measures or indicators that recipients of funding are expected to report against.
3. To demonstrate the impact of the work on society or the economy more generally.
4. To focus and align work with societal challenges or what matters to people or communities.

All of these imperatives can cause challenges for organisations, especially those who need to align themselves with, or be accountable to, multiple outcome frameworks. In our experience, these pressures can be felt acutely by organisations of all different sizes.

The pressures of working to multiple outcome frameworks

Local government – planners and performance managers need to be able to plan for and report against outcomes and indicators specified by multiple government departments, some of which may be directly in competition with one another. For example, targets around economic growth may be at odds with efforts to combat climate change.

Providers of care and support – can have contracts to deliver the same service across multiple local government areas with separate outcomes and indicators for each contract, while also needing to report to care regulators.

Small non-profit organisations – experience tensions when relying on small pots of funding from many different funders and need to report separately to each. For example, an organisation we work with has three different sources of funding for one cookery course and needs to find a way to report to each funder about the separate funder-defined outcomes of this resource.

Research organisations – who are expected to report on the impacts of their work within predefined institutional cycles in order to sustain funding, even though the evidence says it can take years for research to have an impact and that it is unpredictable.

Lots of time and effort can be spent negotiating these competing demands. All too often, organisations find themselves constantly reacting to these wider outcomes and outcome-accountability demands. Sometimes the influence of funders' and decision makers' outcomes can overshadow what originally mattered to the organisation and the people they care about. As discussed in Chapter 3, this can then start to shape the practice and culture of using data and evidence in an organisation – focusing on what funders ask for, rather than what organisations need to understand their own work.

Escaping multiple outcome demands by owning your outcomes

It is possible for organisations to get out of this cycle of constantly responding to other people's outcomes and start owning their own. Organisations like the ones we support, who have done the work to reassess, define and own their outcomes, make significant gains. They get a refreshed, clear and shared vision of how their work makes the difference they want. They gain insight into how the different aspects of their work contribute to their outcomes. They get on top of their data and evidence and are able to balance their own need for data and information alongside requirements to report to others. What is more, they are able to tell a good story of the difference their work makes. This brings many benefits, including increased confidence in the work at every level of the organisation, better decision making and greater influence, as the following case study shows.

Case study of WHALE Arts

WHALE Arts is a creative anchor organisation for a large urban part of Edinburgh that experiences multiple disadvantages. By offering free or low-cost creative activities for young people and adults, they aim to be the creative heart of a vibrant, thriving community. This ranges from a weekly Friday art club, a popular street arts programme and support with digital skills to a free community meal.

WHALE Arts started working differently with outcomes as part of a project funded by the Edinburgh Community Health Forum. All of the organisations in the forum spent time mapping out how their work contributes to improving the health and wellbeing of the communities they care about. (This process is described in more detail in Chapter 6.)

Through this process, the leaders of WHALE Arts realised that they could take control of their outcomes. They spent more time mapping all of their activities across their work to the outcomes that mattered to them as an organisation.

They redefined outcomes from their programmes to be:

Our people are happier.
Our people have improved wellbeing and are more resilient.
Our people are more highly skilled.

These are all self-defined outcomes. In addition to these they revised the outcomes from their partnership work to be:

Our people have better economic prospects.
Clear pathways for creative skills development are available to community members, artists, designers, makers and professionals.
Creative approaches/interventions are highly valued and well funded.
Health inequalities policy and strategy in Edinburgh is informed by the experiences and expertise of our community and partner organisations.

The chief executive of WHALE Arts said: "I hope it will move us away from thinking about our data only in relation to what we report to funders. I think that too many third-sector orgs collect data for their funders and not for themselves. I've been calling this 'owning our outcomes'" (Leah Black, 2021).

There are real advantages to taking the time to redefine outcomes around what matters to the organisation. First, it prevents the need to run after every funding call – instead, it is easier to see how organisation outcomes do or don't align with funders' outcomes, and to focus efforts where there is strong read-across and more likelihood of success. That also means that, if successful, the work will be strongly aligned to the organisation's work and won't result in mission creep. Second, we have found that many good funders and decision makers are happy to flex their outcome-reporting requirements when presented with outcomes that are well defined and evidenced by organisations themselves. This means that reporting to multiple funders can be streamlined into one approach and saves having to create different reports with different data for each funder. It can help ensure that any partnerships or funding arrangements organisations develop are aligned with these outcomes. Overall, this helps organisations to become more robust, sustainable and effective as they focus on what matters to them and don't bend to adapt to what others see as important without careful consideration about what it means to them as an organisation.

Over the coming chapters we will share our approach that many organisations have used to effectively define and own their outcomes, like the example of WHALE Arts. First, we want to take some time to unpick some of the ways of thinking about outcomes that are helpful to explore if you want to be able to put this into practice. This next section takes a tour of some of the principal ideas, including defining what is meant by 'outcomes', what outcomes mean at different levels and busting some myths about outcome approaches.

An introduction to outcome thinking

We know from many years of working with organisations on their outcomes that getting to grips with outcomes and impacts can be hard. Indeed, this was identified by the World Bank as a key barrier to implementing more outcome-based ways of working across public services (Cook, 2017). As already highlighted, we also know that for many people working in public services, the imperative to talk about and work to outcomes or impacts is relatively new. As a result, confidence and practice in outcomes varies considerably. People working in health and social care in Scotland or Wales are likely to be steeped in the language of outcomes. There are other sectors which the language of outcomes and impacts has been slower to reach. Regardless of the level of familiarity, we find it is always helpful to start with a clear definition.

What we mean by an outcome

The first challenge in owning your outcomes is being really clear on what an outcome is, and how this differs from an output. Outcomes are most simply defined as **the changes resulting from a specific service or intervention** (Glendinning et al, 2006). Outcomes can be identified at the start of a process to show what it aims to achieve, and be evaluated at the end of a process (or during it) to understand the difference made. Some evaluators like to differentiate outcomes from impacts, with outcomes relating to the immediate difference that an intervention has made and impacts reflecting longer term changes. In practice, we find this level of differentiation to be rarely meaningful, which is why we use the terms interchangeably.

Outcomes (or impacts if that is your preference) are often conceptualised as coming at the end of a chain of events that starts with an activity and involves processes which generate an output, which in turn contributes to an outcome. Within our work at Matter of Focus, we often use the following diagram (Figure 4.1) to bring these steps in the process to life (first used by the Social Policy Research Unit at the University of York in 2005, adapted by Cook and Miller (2012)).

This visual is a helpful reminder that when talking about outcomes, it is the happy child that is important, not the cake. This can be a 'light bulb' moment for people whose organisations are much more focused on outputs rather than outcomes. It doesn't matter how many cakes (insert your equivalent here) an organisation bakes; if they don't reach the child, are delivered on the wrong day, or are inedible, they won't make the difference hoped. Keeping the outcome (the happy child) firmly in mind helps with navigating the plethora of small decisions that go into any kind of public service delivery, policy or practice influencing, or other change processes.

This example reminds us that, in the real world, the relationships between outputs and outcomes are often not linear and direct. While a lovely birthday cake might contribute to a child feeling happy on their birthday, it is just part of the picture,

Figure 4.1: Showing the relationship between inputs, processes, outputs and outcomes

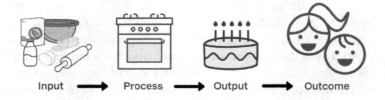

Input ⟶ Process ⟶ Output ⟶ Outcome

and with all complex people-based change, it is multiple factors working together that make the difference. Just as it is the cake, friends and family, and opportunities for play that together are required for a happy child, the outcomes of any work emerge from the interaction of many different factors. This insight has fundamental implications about how to approach work with outcomes that are often not well understood. Rather than thinking that outcomes can be simply achieved, delivered or measured, it is much more realistic to think about them as guiding lights or frameworks for action.

Outcomes (or impacts) as a framework for action

As highlighted earlier in the chapter, outcomes or impacts can be identified at the start of an initiative to show what it aims to achieve. They can be evaluated at the end of (or during) a process to understand the difference made. Used in either way, taking the time to plan for and assess progress towards outcomes can provide a helpful framework for action, which helps these initiatives in a number of ways.

A focus on outcomes can:

- **Build a clear and shared vision of the envisaged change.** This is vital at every level of working and is critical to partnership working (Cook, 2015).
- **Shape a plan of how to work together to make change.** A focus on outcomes gives initiatives a starting point to agree a logical (though not necessarily linear or simplistic) understanding of how planned activities will contribute to the difference hoped for. Breaking down the change process into meaningful steps enables agreement on the contributions of everyone involved and how they expect to get there.
- **Help track progress towards the outcomes that are important.** When delivering people-based services and programmes to address complex social issues, change always takes time and often involves dealing with and responding to the unexpected, both good and bad. A meaningful outcomes framework provides something tangible to anchor work to, track progress against, and helps flex plans as required. It can

help to see when and where progress is slow and give tools for regrouping around what matters.

- **Structure reflections and capture learning.** Sharing and reflecting on learning and telling the story of complex change processes can be hard, especially when organisations want to capture what went well and where things were challenging. Having a clear framework for how work could hopefully contribute to outcomes provides structure for making sense of what happens. It also helps with collecting, collating and analysing data and feedback. It provides the foundation for telling a realistic story that others can learn from, giving space to highlight the unique contribution that individuals and organisations made towards the changes that were realised. This is a process that takes time, but when done well can structure and guide conversations and the kinds of reflective practice that are critical to making change.

Working in a deliberate and focused way with the outcomes that are important to any work can help realise all of the benefits above, but first it is useful to think a bit more about how to define outcomes that focus on the right level for the right people.

Outcomes at different levels

This way of understanding outcomes (or impacts, goals or results) is really helpful for understanding the intentional change as well as changes that emerge. The power of thinking in terms of outcomes is that it is a concept that works at every level of the system. Change can happen at different levels, with a focus on different kinds of people in the system. A primary challenge for organisations looking to own their outcomes is that the same term is used to describe subtly different processes operating at different levels.

We can conceptualise outcomes at the following levels, as summarised in Figure 4.2. At each of these levels, outcomes may be intended or may emerge that relate to the impact of the work on end users and on the initiative or team itself. Thinking through which level is most appropriate for any work is key in defining outcomes for any change programme.

Figure 4.2: Different levels of outcomes

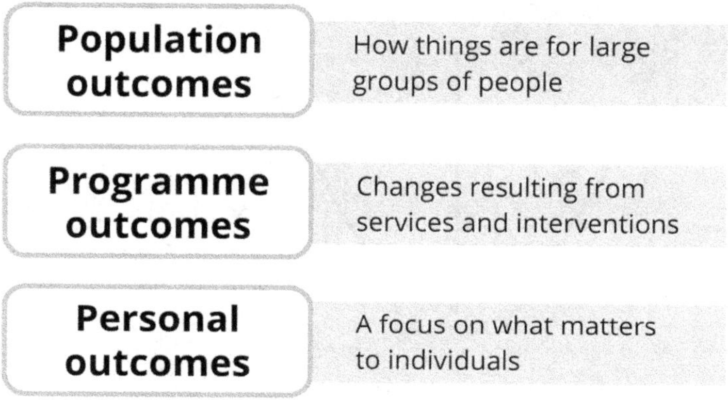

Population outcomes	How things are for large groups of people
Programme outcomes	Changes resulting from services and interventions
Personal outcomes	A focus on what matters to individuals

The term **programme outcomes** relates to the kind of outcomes discussed so far – those outcomes intended or emergent from a specified initiative. The bigger and more complex the work, the harder it will be to understand the difference this work makes to outcomes or impacts. However, this will always be possible with the right approach and sufficient resources, as outlined in this book.

Many national and local organisations also refer to outcomes when they are describing or measuring how things are for their population. **Population outcomes** are not outcomes in the truest sense of the word as they are not directly linked to any specific activity or intervention. Instead, they are a description of how things are for people living in this place/country, or how the government would like them to be. As such, the impact of specific programmes of work on population outcomes can't be evaluated simply; however, it is possible to make a theoretical case for how a programme of work has contributed to population outcomes. This is summarised in Figure 4.3.

Personal outcomes describe the things that matter to a person. Taking a 'personal outcomes approach' (such as the Talking Points approach; see Cook and Miller (2012)) involves having a good conversation with the person exploring their hopes for the future and creates a plan for how this can be achieved, drawing on the person's own assets as well as formal supports where needed.

Figure 4.3: Linking population and programme outcomes

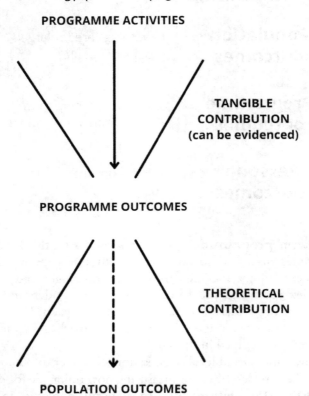

PROGRAMME ACTIVITIES

TANGIBLE CONTRIBUTION (can be evidenced)

PROGRAMME OUTCOMES

THEORETICAL CONTRIBUTION

POPULATION OUTCOMES

Personal outcomes are distinct from the outcomes for individuals of a programme or intervention, which may or may not be things that matter to a person. For example, going to a day centre may increase a person's social contact, but not with people they value spending time with. Understanding the difference a service or support has made to personal outcomes at an individual level is relatively straightforward. Organisations can get this information by talking to the people involved. However, understanding the difference that services or supports make to groups of service users is much harder, as we heard in Chapter 3 – simple measures are not appropriate for these kinds of complex change.

If an organisation needs to be able to speak to population or personal outcomes, being clear about these differences is vital, not least because the kinds of approaches that are appropriate for knowing they are making a difference to programme outcomes are not appropriate for assessing progress towards personal or population outcomes. We discuss some of the implications for this and possible solutions below.

Some common myths about outcomes

The discussion so far about outcomes highlights some of the problems with common assumptions about outcomes – that they can be confusing, overly simplified, and that multiple frameworks overlap. In our work, we help organisations spot and bust common myths about outcomes and impacts. Some we come across regularly are illustrated in Figure 4.4.

Figure 4.4: Outcome myths vs reality

MYTH	REALITY
We deliver outcomes	People deliver pizzas, not outcomes! Outcomes are always the product of lots of different factors and emerge through any work. Delivering outcomes presumes a level of control that doesn't exist in the messy world of public services. Instead, it is possible to assess progress towards outcomes, in a way that recognises the contributions of many different people and factors to this.
We have met our outcomes	Outcomes are fundamentally about change and therefore dynamic. While it is possible to make progress towards an outcome, outcomes are rarely met in a meaningful sense. There is always more that can be done towards the change. This is why it is important to regularly review outcomes and ensure they really reflect what is most important now.
We need a standard approach to delivering outcomes	As the cake example shows, when working in a complex environment, every person or situation is different. Just as every person in your family will choose a different way to celebrate their birthday, so initiatives always need to be tailored to the people and context involved.
We can be accountable for outcomes	When working in a complex system, there are always limits to what can be controlled. Wider factors will always interact with any initiative to influence outcomes, so it isn't meaningful to account for outcomes. Instead, it can be helpful to hold organisations to account for following a careful process towards outcomes.

So, taking all these myths and challenges into account, is it still worth focusing on outcomes? Of course we think so, which is why we have written this book. In the final section of this chapter, we set out some ways of shifting the thinking on outcomes to make this a reality.

A new way of working with outcomes

As you will have gathered already, we believe in the power of outcome or impact thinking to support organisations to make the best difference possible and to know the difference they make. We recognise that for organisations working in this way there are two sets of tensions or challenges to navigate:

1. the challenge of reorientating their organisation and systems to work well with outcomes;
2. the challenge of working within a wider system that can pose unrealistic outcome or impact demands.

We firmly believe that things don't have to be this hard and that many of the problems organisations experience in navigating outcomes come from applying the wrong conceptual or methodological tools for the job. We would like to see public services shift to new ways of thinking for outcomes that recognise the complexity of people-based change and what that means for how organisations, programmes, initiatives and even governments need to respond. This shift is summarised in Figure 4.5.

What's more, we're not the only people who feel this way, and we are delighted to be part of a movement towards more complexity-informed ways of working with outcomes at every level of the system. For example, in Scotland, the Personal Outcomes Network champions meaningful outcome practice. Internationally, the Centre for Public Impact is leading the way in calling for new approaches to working with outcomes strategically and with funders. (See the References section for links to more information.)

Though the potential for system change is exciting, for many organisations we work with, owning their outcomes in the short term means straddling old and new thinking – anchoring

Figure 4.5: New thinking for outcomes

OLD THINKING	NEW THINKING
See change as simple	See change as complex
Deliver or achieve outcomes	Make progress towards outcomes
Success defined and measured by system	Success defined by people and communities involved
Standardised approaches to delivery	Delivery bespoke to context and people
Attribute change to specific initiatives	Highlight the contribution of initiatives
Define or require outcomes	Continually adjust or renegotiate outcomes
Accountable for delivering outcomes	Accountable for careful process informed by outcomes

their own practice firmly in the futures while being able to meet the requirements of old thinking that still exists in the system. Understanding the different assumptions and tensions between the two worlds is an important first step towards better outcome working.

Owning your outcomes: what this means in practice

Owning your outcomes (or impacts) is not only vital for organisations to know what difference they make, it's key to becoming a sustainable and effective organisation and making the best contribution possible to improving outcomes for the people and communities they care about. In our experience, making the move to own outcomes is much easier when underpinned by a clear and coherent understanding of what outcomes, impacts, results and goals are and can be, and what they are not.

Over time, it is easy to spot an organisation that owns their outcomes. These organisations:

* know what matters to the people and communities they care about – what helps and hinders this, what their strengths and assets are and what support is needed to help;

- are clear about what part of these problems their organisation is addressing and how this fits with the contributions of other partners and stakeholders;
- know how they make a difference and what it is about their work that makes this happen;
- have a clear view of how different initiatives and services contribute to their organisational outcomes and how the parts add up to a whole;
- can articulate the fit between their outcomes and the outcomes that matter to funders and decision makers and wider policy goals.

This isn't a one-off exercise; the context in which any initiative works, and the needs and issues people care about, are constantly changing, therefore work needs to change and adapt too. Chapters 5 and 6 outline some practical approaches to get clarity on the context for any work and what this means for outcomes.

Try it yourself

Answer these questions on your own or with your team, to see to what extent your organisation or initiative owns its outcomes. There are links to relevant chapters if you want to improve on any of these.

- Do you have an overarching understanding of how the work of your organisation contributes to outcomes?
- Are you capturing this at different levels?
- Are you clear about the mechanisms that underpin your work?
- Can you articulate how your outcomes connect to funder and policy outcomes?

To improve any of these, try outcome mapping, as set out in Chapter 6.

- Do you reflect on progress towards outcomes and use this to adapt the way you work? (To improve this, see Chapter 8.)

- Do you have feedback data and evidence to underpin the outcomes that matter? (To improve this, see Chapter 7.)
- Are you ready to adapt and respond to the ways you work as the context and systems change? (To think more about this, see Chapter 5.)

5

Embrace the complex context

So much of what differentiates a good organisation from a great one is the ability to understand and work well with the context.

Whether supporting people to move on in their lives, implementing new policy initiatives, providing training or spreading good practice, the evidence shows that the most effective approaches are those that are tailored to the specific context in which the work is done (Cook, 2015). This is something we see in practice every day in our work with organisations, and something that is at the core of understanding the difference they make.

Previous chapters have already outlined how working in complex systems means there are many dynamic and moving parts, and that outcomes or impacts can be unexpected and unpredictable. We discussed in Chapter 2 how the very specific context – the time, place, people, culture, institution and setting – make a huge difference to how things are done and what difference they make. The unpredictability of the COVID-19 pandemic is one example of how context cuts across the delivery of projects, programmes and policies. It's easy to think of other examples at different scales, such as staff recruitment, local or national policy decisions, buildings and infrastructure, and even the weather, that influence the progress of any initiatives.

In our work, we support people to deliberately embrace the complex context for their work. Rather than ignoring it, trying to work well with the challenges and opportunities of any initiative's context can help improve delivery and really make a difference to people and communities. It's also essential for shaping how the initiative will make a difference, and for tracking that difference.

This chapter:

- discusses why context matters;
- sets out a practical framework to help understand context;
- explains why it is important to link context and outcomes with risks and assumptions.

We hope this chapter will help you realise the benefits of embracing the complex context for the work you do and give you some practical tools to help work with this complexity despite the challenges it presents. These practical tools are illustrated with a case study and with examples throughout the chapter.

Why context matters

The most effective public service interventions always attend to context and are appropriately different every time; in other words, tailored to the context they are in.

The contexts in which people live and work are incredibly diverse. What things are like for different people in different settings and places will vary enormously. This is not new but is something that isn't always embraced. It can be easier to focus on the work one organisation or initiative is delivering than to embrace the complex world where the work happens. But when working to deliver and evaluate complex, people-based change, it's always important to pay attention to the interlocking and fluid factors, beyond the direct control of the initiative, which influence how change happens.

Acknowledging that context varies, and that this matters for how initiatives are developed and delivered, is something of a political hot potato – talk of 'postcode lotteries' (Whitebloom,

2020) is common in the news, based on the belief that every citizen is entitled to exactly the same service regardless of where they live.

Further thinking reveals that all initiatives, even national ones, will vary at several levels:

- **Macro:** the particular geographies, histories and structures vary from place to place, meaning delivery will be different.
- **Meso:** the specific configuration of institutions, organisations and infrastructure varies within localities.
- **Micro:** the specific people, place, time, temperature, and so on varies. The people in the room will affect what and how anything is delivered.

Identifying, logging and monitoring the most important of these differences, alongside unforeseen changes that will impact on any initiative, means it is possible to try to work with them rather than be affected by this unpredictability. To do this, it is necessary to think deeply about both the contextual factors that shape any work and the underlying change mechanisms that programmes, projects and services rely on.

This chapter shares the tools we have been using and refining with the organisations we work with. We have applied these to small voluntary sector projects, to medium-sized programmes and to large city or region-wide endeavours. While there will always be room for improvement, we believe these tools are fit for purpose for people who are trying to work well with these contextual factors and get on with the job of delivering.

Deeper dive: how can we work better with systems?

As discussed in Chapter 2, public sector initiatives tend to focus on complex problems embedded in complex systems. These complex systems are characterised as having many interactions between people and place, with multiple projects, programmes and interventions overlapping one another. Policies and practices, past and present, play out across the system. Information, data and stories travel rapidly, and it can be hard to predict what will happen in the future as that is influenced by internal and external factors.

It's important to acknowledge and steer work within these complex systems. Focusing on long-term outcomes can really help provide a sense of direction. In Chapter 2, we set out how a learning culture, effective use of data and evidence, and strong leadership are important.

But working with complex systems also requires acknowledgement of this complexity and how it might affect any specific initiative. This chapter explains how addressing the context is the first step in trying to work with multiple interlocking factors that make up the system in which any work takes place. Analysing and embedding the many contextual factors that will influence the work is vital in helping work in complex settings. It is a way of getting to grips with and managing the characteristic uncertainty of complex work (Patton, 2011).

The benefits of taking time to work with context

Taking time to talk about and analyse context and how this shapes practice and decision making is a powerful way of emphasising the unique contribution an organisation, and the people in it, make to improving outcomes. In our experience, teams find this process enjoyable, validating and even cathartic.

It has practical benefits too. It can help:

- identify key risks to any work;
- think through how risks can be mitigated and build on opportunities to improve or strengthen the way initiatives are delivered;
- establish reasonable expectations about what might be achieved given the time and resources available and contextual opportunities and limitations;
- focus on the contribution to change that any work can make in the context of the system.

Finally, analysing and reflecting on context is widely recognised as being important grounding for any robust theory-based evaluation process. For example, the Canadian Government

Guidance (2021) says, good theory-based evaluation reports start with an account of the context in which the work was carried out and will reflect on the impact of contextual factors (risks and assumptions) throughout the process.

A practical framework to help understand context

In our work, we use the 'ISM framework' (Darnton and Horne, 2013) as a launchpad for talking about and analysing context. This framework, created for the Scottish Government, is evidence based and identifies factors that arise in individual, social and material contexts that are important to consider when setting up or evaluating any initiative. These factors are shown in Figure 5.1.

The framework was developed originally to help organisations plan effective, complexity-informed environmental behaviour change projects. We have found it to be applicable to public

Figure 5.1: The ISM model adapted from Darnton and Horne (2013)

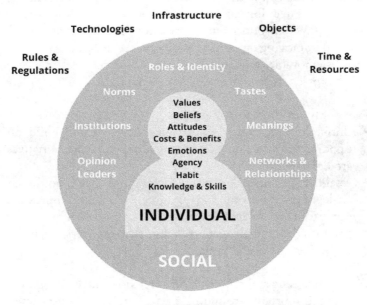

service projects and programmes more generally and have adapted it for wider application.

We found this approach useful for several reasons. It is an evidence-based framework that simply but effectively breaks down contextual factors into the three levels of individual, social and material. Previous work had shown that there is much discussion of context but fewer tools to analyse it (Morton, 2012). Tools that were used by researchers, such as the RAPID framework (Crewe and Young, 2002), while useful, were too in depth for people trying to embed this in their daily work.

We find that the ISM framework can be used in lighter and deeper ways that are suited to different situations and applications. Our usual approach is to use the headings as triggers for group discussion about the factors that will help or hinder any initiative. This can help to:

- prompt discussion and reflection among teams about how contextual factors help their work and what might get in the way;
- organise and analyse data and information from a range of sources that help to understand how contextual factors are shaping any work: meeting notes, consultation findings, reflections from staff teams or evidence from previous research.

Throughout this chapter you will find several examples of context analysis in action, demonstrating how various organisations have adopted the ISM model to understand how context affects their work. By undertaking this work, organisations, projects and programmes can focus on what is important, identify risks and assumptions, highlight what might get in the way of success, and effectively embed their work in the context in which they find themselves, in a real and tangible way.

ISM in action

Here are three examples of how different organisations have used the ISM model and what they gained from taking time to understand and act on contextual influences on their work.

Justifying resources in ethnic minority health

Lothian Minority Ethnic Health Inclusion Service supports people from black and minority ethnic backgrounds, asylum seekers and refugees. Their work is very challenging, with many factors impacting on their work, such as:

- high levels of deprivation and poverty;
- barriers to accessing employment;
- a hostile immigration environment;
- lack of quality interpretation services;
- lack of cultural competence among health and care professionals;
- the specific attitudes and beliefs of people they work with.

Taking time to systematically analyse their context in relation to the ISM framework highlighted to the team just how challenging their work is and how unique and unrecognised many of the challenges they face are. Going through this process helped them build a strong case for the continued existence of a specialist team to fulfil this role.

Setting realistic expectations for changing residential care

The My Life My Way pilot led by East Renfrewshire Health and Social Care Partnership sought to improve outcomes for people in residential care through embedding more choice and control.

Taking time to do an ISM analysis at the start of the evaluation process surfaced the many factors that shaped why it was so hard to improve outcomes for people in residential care. This was important in setting realistic expectations about what the pilot could achieve in the time available.

Doing the right thing – better dementia training for carers

Age Scotland were funded to deliver dementia training to a range of groups including unpaid carers.

At the start of the project, the team used the ISM framework to analyse the context into which their training was being delivered, drawing on learning from planning sessions with unpaid carers. This process highlighted that in many local contexts, adequate services and support weren't in place for unpaid carers.

The team reflected that if they just delivered training to unpaid carers on their rights as planned, they wouldn't make the difference they hoped for. Therefore, they built a community around their training, providing information to people over time and systematically capturing learning from the training sessions to inform Age Scotland's campaigning work.

In each of the three examples discussed, it is clear that ignoring the context would have presented risks to the projects, and that taking time to analyse and understand gave gains in terms of being able to deliver more efficiently and effectively. In our experience, people also find conversation and reflection on context empowering and enjoyable! It is also the starting point for embedding these important factors in understanding if an initiative is making a difference.

Linking context and outcomes with risks and assumptions

It is usual, when trying to understand how an initiative makes a difference, to spend time thinking about the assumptions that underpin it and the risks associated with it (Weiss, 1998). People working with our approach generally start by undertaking a context analysis using the ISM framework, before setting out a theory of change. (We describe this in the next chapter.) Context analysis is useful in thinking about what should be done. It can then be used to identify risks and assumptions, which is an essential part of delivery, helping to manage uncertainty and collect better data on the most significant factors that might influence the work.

The approach described in this book builds on contribution analysis, as discussed in Chapter 2. Contribution analysis starts by setting out how the project intends to work, and what outcomes are important to it (Mayne, 2008). This is a positive vision of how the people who designed the project, programme or policy think and hope it is going to make a difference, based on their experience, the evidence or other factors. Context analysis helps to ground this positive vision in the real world – by identifying what will need to be in place, why people think the initiative will work and the potential risks that it can face. It is essential to consider risks and assumptions when steering any work through its specific complex context.

What are risks and assumptions?

Risks are things that may happen that could get in the way of the change or the outcomes an initiative hopes to see. For example:

- multiple things going on in people's lives that affect their ability to make a positive change;
- inadequate wider services for people to get the support they need;
- staff and resources challenges;
- an external policy change, environmental influence or social challenge that cuts across the work (such as COVID-19).

Assumptions are the change mechanisms at the core of the project and things that need to be in place for an initiative to contribute to the outcomes it seeks. Assumptions include why people think the initiative will unfold in the way that is set out, and what wider factors are important. These might be based on experience of delivering something similar, learning from other initiatives, or from research into similar work. For new and innovative work, testing assumptions is even more important as there may not be an existing evidence base to draw on.

Assumptions may include:

- There is sufficient time and resources for staff to be able to work with people in the way that works for them.
- Staff have the knowledge and skills to deliver this kind of support.
- There are adequate other services, policies, partnerships and initiatives to support the work.
- If **this** happens, then **that** is likely to happen.

Interrogating the assumptions underpinning the theory behind a programme or service brings two main benefits. First, it makes any evaluation more rigorous, linking different levels of outcomes and enabling data to be collected to make stronger claims about the relationship between the programme activities and outcomes (Bicket et al, 2020). Second, and very much in line with our ethos, working with assumptions can be an important source of learning for those delivering the programme, giving deeper insight into how different aspects of the service interact, the impact of context and, critically, what can be improved (Archibald et al, 2016).

When looking at wider risks and assumptions, it is often possible to flip them. (For example, the risk "We can't reach the right people" may be reworded as an assumption: "We reach the right people.") In some cases, they fall more squarely into a risk or assumption category. To be pragmatic, it's best not to worry too much about this: what matters is that they are recorded in a way that makes sense to the work. The most important risks and assumptions need to be considered and included in the way the initiative is monitored and evaluated.

Nearly every initiative working with complex change faces challenges around engagement; it's essential to engage the right people with the work, but often a risk is that people who are easy to deliver to, or who are not ready for the initiative, get the service instead. This is true for service provision, staff training, partnership working and large-scale projects.

If engagement goes wrong, then the initiative probably won't contribute to its intended outcomes or make the difference it hoped. So, it's important to pay close attention to understanding the people at the heart of any work and how they are feeling. This is explored further in the next chapter.

Bringing context and risk together for action

By analysing context – and revisiting that analysis regularly – risks and assumptions can be identified and included in planning, reviewing progress, learning and explaining where the work has made a contribution. Completing an ISM analysis brings focus to the elements of the context that will have the biggest impact on the work. Initially focusing on the main contextual risks and assumptions, and then on internal risks and assumptions, provides a solid foundation from which to understand, mitigate, learn, improve and make a difference.

Once risks and assumptions are clear for a project, what next?

- A team delivering an initiative can regularly reflect and review them to help steer in the right direction.
- When risks emerge or accelerate, or assumptions become shaky, it is easier to take action quickly to minimise the impact on the initiative, or change direction if needed.
- Risks and assumptions can form the basis for data collection – in feedback forms, interviews or other data. This is a good way of testing them as the work unfolds.

How to test assumptions and monitor risks

Testing assumptions and monitoring risks can be done simply and easily within a framework for evaluation, as we set out in Chapter 6. This usually involves ranking assumptions and risks in order of importance; that is, the riskiest risks and the least safe assumptions first. Testing these involves intentionally seeking out data, evidence and feedback that will show if the risks are emerging, or if the assumptions are playing out as intended.

Most people-based change makes an assumption that any initiative can identify and reach the people intended as beneficiaries of the work. This assumption is usually based on experience of engaging similar types of people before. To test this assumption, data needs to be collected that shows the people engaged are the target and not people easier to reach, or just a subset of intended recipients. What this looks like will vary depending on the work. For example, reaching all social work directors might be simpler and easier to test than identifying the most vulnerable families in a community. Whatever the risk or assumption, asking "How will you know if you are successful?" can help frame the data, evidence or feedback needed to test it.

The following case study illustrates this in action.

Case study: Understanding the opportunities in ending violence against children in Peru

This case study sets out how the approach described in this chapter was used to understand the impact of work to influence policy on violence against children in Peru. It shows how the ISM was used as a framework to analyse context and then take that learning to develop and test risks and assumptions.

A team of researchers from UNICEF and the University of Edinburgh were trying to understand the impact of their research on reducing violence against children (Morton and Casey, 2017). They had carried out a multicountry project, working closely with policy makers and practitioners in Peru to help them apply data and evidence to the issues. They used the ISM to help frame their contribution and highlight the key risks and assumptions.

ISM analysis for action on violence against children in Peru

Individual factors

- People are ashamed of the levels of violence, and of their own experiences as children.
- People think violence is just a part of growing up.
- People don't believe the levels of violence identified.
- People are overwhelmed by the size of the problem.
- There are limited ways of sharing evidence and potential solutions.
- Policy makers are worried about the cost implications of tackling the problem.
- Many people want to do something about levels of violence and want to learn.

Social factors

- Cultural norms of violence, including the view that it is the parents' choice how to raise their children.
- Personal experiences of violence in the past still affect decisions today.

- Corporal punishment is seen as effective discipline by practitioners and institutions.
- Patriarchal norms where men are endorsed for violent behaviour.
- It is a cross-ministerial issue but difficult to work across ministries.
- A groundswell of people who want change.
- Research might not be seen as helpful.
- Government ministries reluctant to undertake or use research.

Material factors

- Abandoned children are at high risk of violence – a much bigger systemic issue than can be tackled by this project.
- Change of government can disrupt action and undermine commitments.
- Lack of support for professionals and parents.
- People need more information about discipline strategies that are non-violent.
- The child protection system is underdeveloped.
- Peru has three distinct geographical regions that need different approaches.
- The potential of the internet and social media for communication, information and support.
- Support for children is being offered by a children's helpline.

Putting the ISM into evaluation

Because the ISM highlighted individual attitudes, interviews included a question that asked people how their own experiences and attitudes had impacted the work. At the social level, the impact study explored civil servants' attitudes to research, and the factors that had helped them develop better data and evidence. The ISM highlighted the multisector nature of the problem and allowed the research impact study to focus on the specific contribution of the project.

The ISM process also highlighted the risk that researchers, government actors and others were affected by the norms around violence against children in very personal ways, and that it was a highly sensitive subject.

This was also backed with research (World Health Organization, 2016). The following risks and assumptions were highlighted as key to test:

Risks

- Violence against children is a sensitive subject that people don't want to talk about.
- There is insufficient trust to allow people to talk about such a sensitive issue.
- It would take too much time to build up trust in this project.

Assumption

- We can provide a neutral platform to talk about violence against children.

These were tested in interviews through the following questions:

- Do you think the study has influenced attitudes to violence against children among colleagues? If so, in what ways?
- Do you think the approach of the research was the best way to understand the drivers of violence affecting children in Peru? By the research approach, I mean collaboration between international and national experts in different fields and from different types of organisations and using qualitative and quantitative research to understand why violence against children occurs in Peru.

Answers to these questions helped to test these risks and assumptions. It was clear through the interviews that the problem is more that people do not recognise violence, or do not recognise it as a problem. Comments in the interviews included, "Violence is normal" and "This problem is so ingrained in our daily lives ... to the point that we do not realise it" (Morton and Casey, 2017).

An academic researcher also said that before the study, violence was not a priority among colleagues at NGOs or other academics. They went on to say that at the policy level, violence was "less visible than it should be but the fact that the government decided to take part in the study was a good sign".

So, while sensitivity was not considered to be an issue, the study taking place was seen to galvanise determination to tackle the invisibility of the problem.

In highlighting what difference this project made to policy change on violence against children it was possible to demonstrate that *the way* the project had been carried out – the careful building of stakeholders across sectors – had been fundamental to its impact. This had been an untested assumption before the data was collected.

Conclusions

In our work with organisations and initiatives, we have seen the power of working with context by deliberately identifying, analysing and including contextual factors that might influence the work. We have shown how this was important to different projects – helping them focus on what matters to them, to change direction when needed, to talk to funders and stakeholders if they need to change direction, and to illustrate *how* they made a difference.

It is clear that highlighting some of the hidden effort that goes into these kinds of interventions and helping to showcase the specific contribution made can benefit complex work. Like some of the other work we outline in this book, while it is beneficial to take the time and effort to work in this way, often time for planning, reflecting and learning is seen as expendable in the hurry to deliver more and better. There is a contradiction in that use of resources – if people in public service are to deliver better in complex environments, they need the time to plan and reflect and work well with the complex contexts they encounter. In the following chapters we build on this discussion, by describing how to set out what difference any initiative makes, and ways of collecting and using the data needed to demonstrate impact.

Try it yourself

You can download our guide to using the ISM framework here: https://www.matter-of-focus.com/understand-the-uni que-context-of-your-work/

There are a few different ways you could then use this guide – for discussion, for full analysis, for wider consultation. This is how we usually do it:

- Get together a team of key people and, if possible, others who understand the work (not directly involved but who understand and care about it – partner organisations, referrers, advisors, etc.).
- Use the prompts in the ISM model to discuss the contextual factors. We usually make two lists under each heading (individual, social and material) – one for enablers of success and another for barriers.
- Once this brainstorm is complete, sort and rank the lists.
- See if you can pick three barriers (risks) and three enablers (assumptions) to include when you collect feedback about your work.

6

Clarify the change you want to see

Working with initiatives that are trying to tackle some of the most difficult problems society faces can be challenging. As we have already discussed, when working with people – whether empowering, educating, inspiring, supporting or collaborating with them – initiatives often have a sense of what they are trying to do, and sometimes one or more outcome they are working towards. These outcomes might come from funders, the organisational mission, the Sustainable Development Goals or national frameworks, and, as we said in Chapter 4, it is easy to get caught in a tangle of outcomes.

While goals and outcomes can usefully give a sense of direction and the bigger picture, what is often missing is clarity of *how* what is being delivered might contribute to the outcomes or impacts that matter.

A meaningful connection between activities and outcomes is often vague or unexplored – but this magic 'how' change happens is essential for driving programmes and for understanding their impact.

Outcome or impact maps are the core of the approach in this book, as the building block for setting out, understanding, learning about and evidencing change. This is one type of 'theory of change' approach which is common for understanding change in complex systems. We believe that process-driven theories of change are most effective for public services, and in this chapter we set out our version of this – outcome or impact mapping – and illustrate how it can be used at different levels.

This chapter discusses:

- thinking about whether and how something makes a difference: an introduction to theories of change and outcome mapping;
- the key components of an outcome or impact maps;
- what is different about this approach;
- the role of pathways in understanding change;
- outcome mapping at different levels: project, programme, organisation or partnership;
- bringing an outcome or impact map to life with risks and assumptions.

This chapter builds on the concepts introduced earlier in this book – especially Chapter 4 on working with outcomes and clarifying your contribution – but also with the challenge of making services more fit for the complex world of delivery. We hope this chapter will give you a very practical way of developing a vision for the change you are working towards and opening up how you think that change will happen.

Illustrated with examples from our work, including a health organisation bringing together staff training and capacity building with delivering front-line services, it will also provide two other case studies of how this has been used by an intermediary organisation and a community-level initiative.

Thinking about whether and how something makes a difference: an introduction to theories of change and outcome mapping

Outcome mapping – or impact mapping, depending on your preference – is an approach that helps to set (or 'map') out the steps that link the activities of a project, programme or organisation to the outcomes that are important. It has a lot in common with other theory of change approaches.

A theory of change is not as grand as it sounds – it's just a term that refers to making explicit the thinking behind why a programme, project or intervention will make a difference to the people or communities it seeks to serve.

There are lots of names for these types of theory-based approaches – logic models, programme theory/logic, results chains, impact pathway analysis, outcome mapping – with key and nuanced differences between them, not always very clearly articulated (Blamey and Mackenzie, 2007; Rogers, 2008; Morton, 2015). Theory-based approaches to evaluation are common at a programme level, setting out the ideas on which any programme is based, or 'the set of beliefs that underlie action' (Weiss, 1998, p 55).

Outcome maps and other theory of change approaches include a statement of the programme's goals and intentions and consider the logic behind how resources and inputs might be linked to outputs, and eventually outcomes and impacts, through a series of logical steps (Weiss, 1998; Morton, 2015; Cook, 2017).

These outcome or impact maps look very different depending on the sorts of projects, programmes or policy change processes. Figure 6.1 is a fictional wellbeing service, which works with adults to support them towards improved wellbeing. We use this example throughout this chapter.

This outcome map simply sets out how the core activities of this project – both supporting people directly and sharing learning – contribute to different levels of outcomes through reactions, learning, behaviour change and the final outcome: people having improved wellbeing.

We explain how we construct an outcome map and the ways that it can be used for understanding change, but in general terms as a framework for evaluation. This means that data collection methods are developed in line with the map, and that sources of evidence can be organised across the map. Using an outcome map like this can demonstrate both how a programme works and how it contributes to outcomes alongside other factors.

Outcome maps can be for single initiatives, programmes, partnerships or linked to show strategy or organisational approaches as we describe in more detail later in this chapter.

Figure 6.1: Example outcome map: a wellbeing service links activities to outcomes

WHAT WE DO	WHO WITH	HOW THEY FEEL	WHAT THEY LEARN AND GAIN	WHAT THEY DO DIFFERENTLY	WHAT DIFFERENCE DOES THIS MAKE?
Have good conversations with people about factors impacting on their wellbeing and what they can do to change	People experiencing poor health and wellbeing	This is a good conversation and I feel ready to make a change	People know what matters to them and have the knowledge, confidence, skills to change	People make changes and actively manage their wellbeing	People have improved wellbeing
We capture learning from our work and share best practice through regular reports	Practitioners in our organisation		Access to a range of relevant community supports and services	People access supports from appropriate agencies	Services are used more appropriately
We develop and deliver training	People who plan and manage services in our organisation and across the local service system	This is for me	Practitioners, planners and managers know what is working well and what can be improved	Practitioners, managers and planners make changes to improve their services	Services are continually improving
We work collaboratively to develop and share resources to support good practice	People who work with the population of interest	People feel this is relevant and important to their role	Practical approaches to work with people and systems to promote health and wellbeing	Deliver effective services and improve practice	People get support to maximise health and wellbeing
We run group sessions					

You know where you are with an outcome map

Outcome maps come into their own when they are used as practical tools. They make explicit what is expected to change, and how this will happen. But they serve several other purposes as well. An outcome or impact map:

- sets out how an initiative seeks to make change;
- brings focus to key activities and how they are linked to change;
- brings people together to build a common understanding of what a project, organisation or partnership is trying to achieve, and what is important;
- streamlines the data and evidence needed to understand an initiative and tell an evidence-based story;
- provides an evaluation framework – helping to define the data needed, questions for data collection and analysis, and a framework for reporting;
- is a simple communication tool and helps to demonstrate the difference an initiative makes to the people and communities that are the focus of the work.

Our outcome mapping approach

For many years, we have been working with organisations with a mission for social change to help them understand and work with outcomes, and we have developed a distinctive approach.

It is no accident that we have pioneered this approach in Scotland, in a setting where the Scottish Government has promoted an outcomes approach to service commissioning and delivery for more than ten years. (See the National Performance Framework in the References section.) Organisations across the public and third sector have been commissioned on outcomes and need to illustrate how what they do contributes to the outcomes that the government defines. This means many organisations are grappling with outcome evaluation challenges.

Outcome approaches are also gaining traction globally, for example through the Sustainable Development Goals (see the References section), which is pushing outcome and impact evaluation up the agenda internationally.

We have built our outcome mapping approach on strong foundations, and we like to think it has great pedigree!

Initially, we developed this approach to working with outcomes for research impact assessment (Morton, 2015). It has been refined and reworked through experimentation and learning with many different kinds and sizes of projects, programmes and organisations. We know that outcome mapping can work well for projects, programmes, partnerships and larger change or improvement initiatives.

The approach is based on contribution analysis, because, as presented in Chapter 2, it is important to use complexity-informed approaches for complex work. Rather than shoehorning simple cause and effect models, contribution analysis reflects and embraces complex and multilayered change.

We built on work by Steve Montague, who took the basic ideas of contribution analysis and turned them into practical approaches (Montague, 2012). This work inspired us to make sure that our model is squarely focused on people – and how change happens between and with people. For this reason, this chapter will include emotions in various ways.

We also brought a strong understanding of outcomes from our work (Cook and Miller, 2012; Cook, 2017). This means finding ways of working meaningfully with outcomes, rather than relying on crass measures, as we talked about in Chapter 3.

Other parts of our experience have been key in how we developed this approach to outcome mapping. If people are going to embrace self-evaluation, and really use an outcome map to drive and understand change, they need to be committed and to buy into the approach. Our participatory ethic (from community education and highlighting lived experience) has been a core component of how we work with people to help them articulate and own their outcome maps. We also use principles from action research, such as action-learning cycles and reflective practice. Finally, we have built on an understanding that people in public services need to combine multiple sources of evidence (from research, administrative data, feedback, reflection, and so on) to understand real-world change programmes. We acknowledge that people are not passive recipients of knowledge; rather, they interact with these different kinds of data and information from their own understanding, and often in conversation, dialogue and discussion with people shaping and using services and programmes (Morton, 2015).

The key components of outcome or impact maps

Over the years we have been working with organisations faced with the challenges of understanding complex work, and have refined a set of headings for outcome mapping (see Figure 6.2). These are very simply expressed, focusing on the processes through which an initiative works, rather than set ideas about time. We have thought very hard about the wording in these headings and in this section we explain a bit more about them.

The simplicity of the headings helps to clarify thinking and make outcome or impact maps accessible as long as they're also written in simple language. This means they can become a communication tool for sharing any initiative's intended activities, outcomes and impacts, which makes it useful for funding applications, partnership discussion or discussing with beneficiaries.

We use a six-step approach, starting with outputs. Any inputs to the initiative are described in the set-up of the model.

Figure 6.2: Our headings for outcome and impact mapping and tracking

What we do

This column describes activities that are delivered as part of the initiative, such as outputs, face-to-face support or services delivered, programmes or training, policy development, research sharing and communication campaigns.

Who with

Who is engaged and involved? This is a simple list of who is important to the success of the initiative. That might be service users, staff, funders, wider stakeholders, partners, civil servants, decision makers, and so on.

How they feel

This step highlights what is needed for positive engagement and is an integral part of this model of change. Putting people at the heart of change means that their engagement is essential and without it no further change will happen. Here, reactions are defined – how do people need to feel in order to be positively engaged with this initiative? This thinking applies equally well to service users, staff, politicians and anyone who needs to be bought into the change process.

What they learn and gain

This refers to changes in knowledge, skills, attitudes or capacities. It highlights the changes that are required for people to act differently. These are sometimes referred to as short-term outcomes but defining them as learning and capacity outcomes helps to focus on the processes that underpin the initiative and sharpens thinking.

What they do differently

This column highlights any changes in behaviour, policy or practice that are important to the initiative. This includes behaviour at the individual level – which is usually the focus of initiatives aimed at people and communities. It also works well when considering policy or practice change, in highlighting what practitioners or policy makers need to do differently to contribute to the outcomes or impacts the initiative is working towards.

What difference does this make?

Here the model asks the 'So what?' question. What will be different in the world? What will be better for people or communities? This can include modest initiative-level outcomes, for example people taking better care of their health. It can also include grander, funders' outcomes: for example, 'people are healthier'. How each initiative uses these outcomes in terms of assessment is discussed later in this chapter and in Chapter 7.

It's not too late!

We have been describing using outcome or impact maps to set out the intended way an initiative will work, but it's not too late if something is already being delivered. Indeed, we have used this approach with many organisations and projects to articulate how they currently do things, or to look back and assess the impact of action already taken.

Setting out an outcome or impact map using these headings, or another approach, is an essential component to understanding and tracking change. It forms the foundations through which change will be understood, adaptations made and learning embedded.

What is different about this approach

This approach aims to be practical but with strong and sound theoretical underpinning to help people working in public services design, deliver and understand the effectiveness of the work they do. This approach to outcome and impact mapping has been tried, tested and refined over many years to put practical tools and sound thinking into the hands of those responsible for addressing some of the trickiest problems society faces. There are a couple of points about how this is different from other similar approaches.

Process focus

The kind of outcome and impact maps created here are process driven. Many initiatives are focused firmly on what they do and are good at articulating the fantastic work they deliver. Most organisation websites clearly state what they do: what services they offer and what initiatives they run. Many organisations have clearly articulated outcomes – Oxfam wants to 'end poverty' – and programmes and projects are commissioned based on outcomes such as reducing food insecurity. So, setting out what initiatives deliver, and what difference they want to make in the world, is relatively easy.

What is more difficult is to explain *how* they make a difference, and that is where a practical, plain language approach like the one set out here can help. Through a process of discussion and deliberation, the framework can be used to drill into how any initiative's activities and outputs contribute to change through a series of logical and transparent steps. This focus on 'how' helps with several aspects of design, delivery and data gathering. It means that people have to think really clearly about how those benefiting and engaging with an initiative need to feel for it to be successful, as well as what learning and capacity building underpins change. Finally, as well as establishing what is expected to change in terms of behaviours, policies or practices, it pushes people to articulate the 'So what?' question: what will be better in the world? In the next chapter we clarify how this same process helps to frame the data, evidence and feedback needed to learn, improve and tell a great impact story.

How is time represented?

If you are used to looking at theories of change or logic models of different kinds, you might be wondering why there are no time frames built into this approach. Often, similar approaches invite the definition of short-term, medium-term and long-term outcomes or impacts. With this approach, however, we don't make any assumptions about time, but instead focus on process. In fact, change can happen across an outcome map or pathway at different times for different groups, and with many feedback loops, obstacles on the way, reiteration and unexpected changes.

There are some real advantages to focusing on process rather than time:

- The focus is on *how* change happens, as well as what.
- There is no need to try to predict the timescales on which change might occur.
- The vision can be really long term – beyond the life of the initiative – but early data will reveal the promise of the approach.

We have found that using this process-led approach really helps people to focus on what is important about their work and set out an outcome or impact map much more easily than when asked solely to map short-, medium- and long-term outcomes. It also embeds a notion of people-based change – when people need to feel engaged and to gain knowledge, skills or capacity, they will behave differently.

Figure 6.3 illustrates some of the ways time might work for our example project. You will see that for what people learn and gain, this might happen at different times, and isn't a one-off event. So, rather than expecting learning outcomes to happen in the short term, this approach is more generous and doesn't expect the ability to predict timescales.

A map of the complex world

The other reason we have included this annotated outcome map is to demonstrate that outcome or impact maps are a representation of much more complex processes. We need to embrace complexity but not be overwhelmed by it. By setting out an outcome or impact map, with risks and assumptions as described in Chapter 5, then it is possible to provide an organising framework for much more complex processes. Although the map looks linear, it represents a non-linear process.

A flexible framework

We cannot emphasise enough that an outcome or impact map should not be seen as a one-off vision of the changes envisaged by an initiative. Given the preceding discussion about complex people-based change, it might seem obvious that these maps should be flexible and adaptable. There are several ways in which they might change over time.

Outcome and impact maps need to be adapted if:

- an unexpected factor means the envisaged change isn't possible;
- further outcomes emerge that were not seen when the map was created;

Figure 6.3: Annotated pathway – demonstrating non-linearity and time

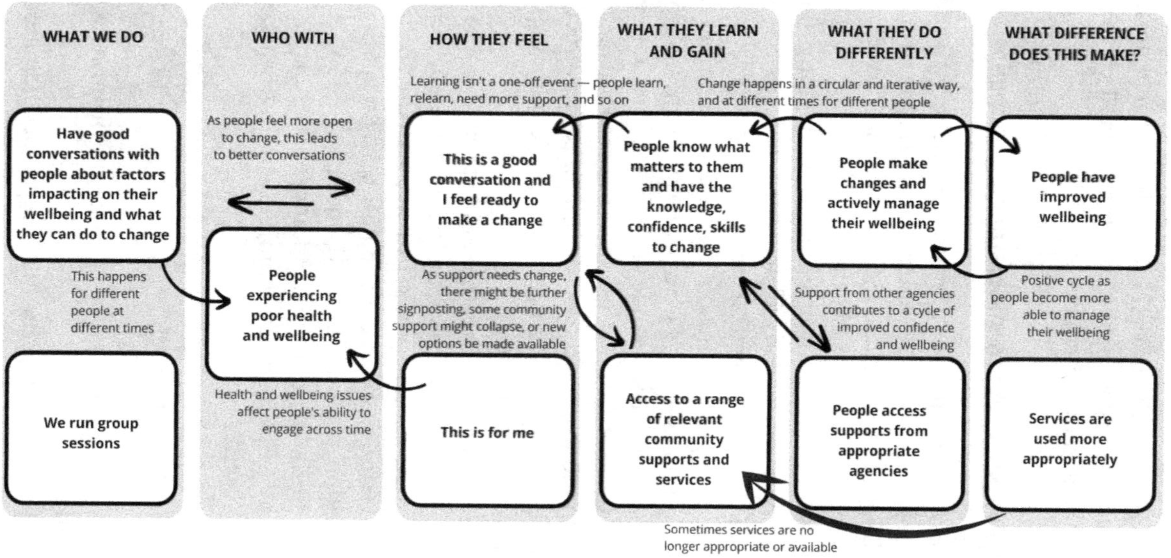

WHAT WE DO

Have good conversations with people about factors impacting on their wellbeing and what they can do to change

This happens for different people at different times

We run group sessions

WHO WITH

As people feel more open to change, this leads to better conversations

People experiencing poor health and wellbeing

Health and wellbeing issues affect people's ability to engage across time

HOW THEY FEEL

Learning isn't a one-off event — people learn, relearn, need more support, and so on

This is a good conversation and I feel ready to make a change

As support needs change, there might be further signposting, some community support might collapse, or new options be made available

This is for me

WHAT THEY LEARN AND GAIN

Change happens in a circular and iterative way, and at different times for different people

People know what matters to them and have the knowledge, confidence, skills to change

Access to a range of relevant community supports and services

Sometimes services are no longer appropriate or available

WHAT THEY DO DIFFERENTLY

People make changes and actively manage their wellbeing

Support from other agencies contributes to a cycle of improved confidence and wellbeing

People access supports from appropriate agencies

WHAT DIFFERENCE DOES THIS MAKE?

People have improved wellbeing

Positive cycle as people become more able to manage their wellbeing

Services are used more appropriately

- some people were not engaged as thought, or other people were engaged;
- data suggests that some of the ideas about change are not right;
- the initiative needs to flex to meet demand or to ensure it keeps focused on outcomes.

The role of pathways in understanding change

Once an outcome map has been created and refined and there is broad agreement that it represents the work, the next task is to think about the key change mechanisms that enable outcomes and impact to occur. We call these pathways.

Occasionally, a pathway contains everything within an outcome map (particularly if the initiative is discrete and well bounded). Usually though, pathways are created to show the different change mechanisms that a project, programme or organisation focuses on. These pathways might be grouped by different stakeholders (people benefiting from a service, and wider professionals); or they might be grouped by type of activity (relating to the work of different teams or programmes); or they can even be grouped by outcome (strategic outcomes for your organisation or policy area).

Pathways then become the units of assessment for data gathering and analysis. Thinking about what evidence is needed to demonstrate each step of a pathway starts to shape a robust evaluation framework. A contribution analysis approach means starting with data already at hand, and then looking to fill gaps, as set out in the next chapter. Adding evidence at each step in the pathway helps understand progress, and assess where data is stronger or weaker.

Why are pathways helpful?

- Pathways focus on the key change mechanisms within any initiative.
- They focus thinking on the specific people, activities and outcomes that are important.
- Pathways help focus on the evidence you need to demonstrate change.

- They provide a way of sharing what was done in a project or programme, and how it was done.
- Pathways make the evaluation process more manageable by establishing discrete units of assessment.

Most outcome or impact maps have two or three pathways, with each representing an impact or contribution story that needs to be told. Focusing on pathways gives more clarity about which stories should be told to which people in a way that feels meaningful and true to the work being done. Pathways can also highlight the shared ways action across different programmes works together to make a difference.

A healthcare improvement agency ran hundreds of change programmes, but when they set out pathways for these, they found that there were five core change mechanisms that underpinned all of their programmes. This meant that they were able to better understand one another's work and could take a streamlined approach to evaluation.

In Figure 6.4, we present the pathways for our example fictional wellbeing service. Two pathways were identified for this map – one focusing on the work supporting people, and the other on how the agency shared its learning in order to improve the system.

In this example there is a different change mechanism for each of these pathways – the work to support people, one-to-one or in groups, creates change by helping individuals define

Figure 6.4: Wellbeing Service outcome map and pathways

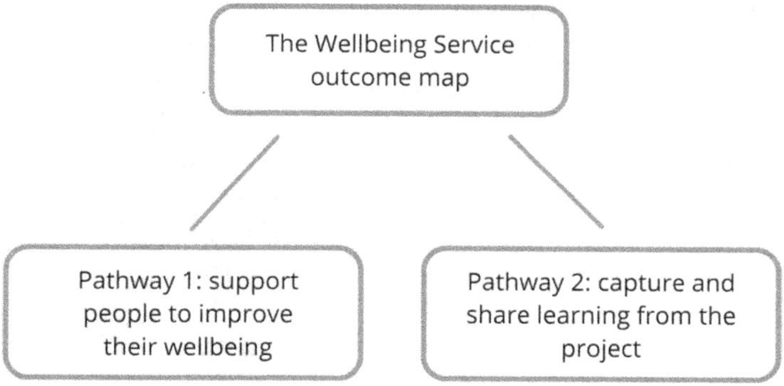

and act on what matters to them (see Figure 6.5). The work to capture and share the learning, through professional training and networks, creates change by shifting the way other services and organisations think about this work, work together and commission differently (Figure 6.6). The pathways meet at the high-level outcomes where they share 'What difference does this make?'

Here, it's reasonably obvious what the pathways should be, but this isn't always the case. We often describe the process of creating a good pathway combination as an art rather than a science! The good thing about that is that there isn't a wrong way of doing it, rather many possible ways. The following tips can help.

Tips for making the best of pathways

We have found through our work defining outcome maps and pathways that the following considerations can help:

- **Balance:** A need to balance what is important to demonstrate about the work with the effort required to generate evidence and monitor progress. The more pathways, the bigger the evaluation job. It is a bit of an art to get this right, but there is plenty of room for experimentation and flexing.
- **Focus on what is distinctive:** It's helpful to identify which activities are distinctive, such as one-to-one support and wider community engagement. These activities are both important – but they are often very different from one another.
- **Highlight innovation:** Pathways can usefully emphasise cutting-edge practice or innovative approaches to care and support. These will also benefit most from data collection, learning and refining that happens at pathway level.
- **Define data needs:** Usually, pathways will use different sources of data, and thinking about the data needed to demonstrate change can be a helpful way of deciding what elements of the work should be in a pathway, or separated out.
- **Case studies:** A pathway is one way to create a case study of a particular aspect of the work.

Figure 6.5: Pathway 1: Support people to improve their wellbeing

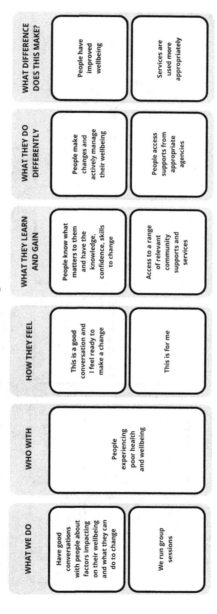

WHAT WE DO

Have good conversations with people about factors impacting on their wellbeing and what they can do to change

We run group sessions

WHO WITH

People experiencing poor health and wellbeing

HOW THEY FEEL

This is a good conversation and I feel ready to make a change

This is for me

WHAT THEY LEARN AND GAIN

People know what matters to them and have the knowledge, confidence, skills to change

Access to a range of relevant community supports and services

WHAT THEY DO DIFFERENTLY

People make changes and actively manage their wellbeing

People access supports from appropriate agencies

WHAT DIFFERENCE DOES THIS MAKE?

People have improved wellbeing

Services are used more appropriately

Figure 6.6: Pathway 2: Capture and share learning from the project

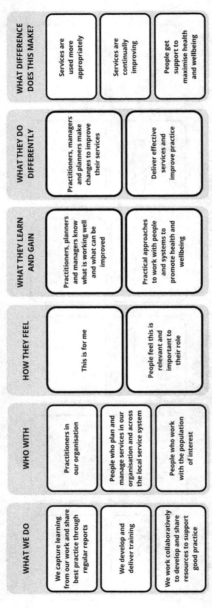

Three ways to organise pathways

There are many possible ways to organise pathways, but here are three common ones:

1. **Who?** Focusing on who is important to the work can highlight different ways of working with people. For example, having a distinct pathway for people accessing support and another for carers and families can show the different ways these particular groups are supported. Or focusing one pathway on policy makers, and another on practitioners.
2. **How?** Focusing on different aspects of activity – such as influencing policy and practice, wider communications work, and building staff capacity, or working directly to support people – can put the spotlight on the different approaches being taken to create change and the way this work leads to outcomes and impact.
3. **So what?** Focusing a pathway around strategic outcomes can show how activity and reach lead to an organisation's, funder's or policy area's top-level outcomes.

There is no one right or wrong way to decide on which pathways will work in any setting – it usually becomes obvious through a process of discussion, trying out and flexing when needed.

The focus on process that is built into outcome mapping and devising pathways means that a discussion of the shared thinking and assumptions behind the design and delivery of any initiative becomes part of the conversation. It puts a clear focus on the people who are important, and what part they play in the changes sought.

Including emotions

Engaging with emotions is critical to effective people-based change. Being explicit about how emotional factors influence change at different levels is important to developing a robust and meaningful outcome map. These include:

- How those engaged in the intervention need to feel to get the benefits and make the changes anticipated. This includes how they need to feel about the intervention itself (is it credible, helpful, the kind of intervention they value?), as well as how they need to feel themselves in order to benefit (am I motivated, hopeful, safe and listened to?).
- The nature of the emotional journey that people need to go on to benefit from a service or play their part in a change programme. This includes emotional gains through the intervention (for example, confidence), how this influences behaviour (acting with confidence) and what difference it makes to their lives (the specific gains for people and communities due to increased confidence).
- The emotional work carried out through the intervention to enable people to respond in the ways they need to, to engage and go on the emotional journey anticipated.
- How factors in the wider context for the programme influence emotional engagement, the emotional journey and the emotion work carried out.

Within our outcome mapping framework, these emotional aspects of change can be made explicit in the 'how they feel' column but will also come to play in the activities undertaken, what people learn and gain, what they do differently and what difference this makes.

Outcome mapping at different levels: project, programme, organisation or partnership

One of the most satisfying aspects of our work with organisations is that we have found this outcome mapping approach relevant to projects, programmes, organisations and partnerships. Of course, it is easiest to map out a new intervention that is well bounded and on a small scale. However, outcome or impact maps are also hugely useful on these other scales too.

Outcome mapping for programmes

Mapping a programme, like other forms of outcome or impact mapping, means making visible the change mechanisms at the heart of the work. This can serve several uses, and pathways are a way of making this work well. Setting out the different aspects of a programme's reach can be done in pathways; for example, one that focuses on benefits for people who are being supported, another pathway to highlight sharing learning in the system.

Getting people together to map a programme of work helps to really understand it and sets a framework for evaluation. In some cases, we have met with people who are working on a programme, and, following outcome mapping, each delivery arm of the programme has tracked their progress on the outcome map. They have then come back together to discuss and evidence shared learning for the programme.

Outcome mapping for organisations

Mapping out all the work an organisation delivers – whatever the organisation – can be a good way to get an overview of that work and, of course, provides ways of tracking progress. The programme approach described above is relevant here as sometimes organisations have programmes or streams of work across the organisation. Some organisations then pull this together into a strategic map (as illustrated in Figure 6.7). This strategic map uses the other maps as data for this organisational viewpoint. It can

Figure 6.7: Nested outcome maps from strategy to project levels

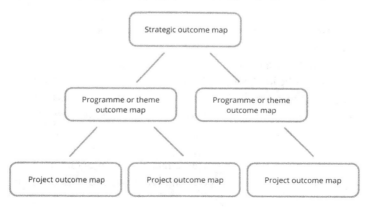

be ambitious to map everything an organisation does, but often starting with one part of the organisation and taking learning from there to other parts is a good way of going about this.

Outcome mapping for partnerships

Outcome mapping is particularly effective for partnerships – coming together to map the overall partnership outcomes and making a pathway for each organisation involved that they can track (Figure 6.8). The pathways consist of activities, engagement and outcomes chosen from the outcome map for each partner. It is then clear what has been delivered by each partner, and how that contributes to the outcomes for the partnership as a whole.

Figure 6.8: Outcome mapping and pathways for a partnership

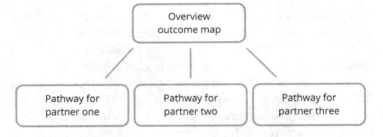

Case study: partnership to address food insecurity

The Tasting Change programme was a partnership between a healthy living centre, a money advice project, an arts organisation, a community food project and a children and families organisation to address food insecurity in the local area. Each partner delivered different aspects of the programme: community events to cook and eat together, advice on budgeting for food, cookery classes, events for children and creative sessions on food.

Together they created an outcome map for the programme. Each organisation then plotted their own data and evidence against a specific pathway. It was agreed that certain data would be collected by every partner, including specific numbers about activities and engagement, and core questions would be asked in feedback forms for every project.

This was brought together to demonstrate the effectiveness of the programme. At the end of the programme they were able to highlight both the contribution of each partner and the overall impact of the programme.

Bringing an outcome map to life with risks and assumptions

An outcome map and pathways represent a version of the positive change an initiative wants to achieve or influence in the world. By nature, they are positive stories of how change hopefully happens. To ground them into the real world, assessing and including the risks and assumptions is important.

This topic is one that external evaluators discuss at length. However, as in other aspects of this approach already set out, we advocate for balancing pragmatism and robustness in work with risks and assumptions. The best outcome or impact-based evaluations will use risks and assumptions right across data analysis and sense making. In real-world settings, the extent and sophistication with which risks and assumptions are embraced within outcome maps will vary considerably in terms of capacity for data collection and analysis, and whether the emphasis is on learning, improvement or testing.

As discussed in the previous chapter, when we are working to deliver complex, people-based change, we need to pay attention to the interlocking and fluid factors, beyond the direct control of the initiative, that influence how change happens.

Considering risks and assumptions for an outcome map or pathway

Once an outcome map and pathways have been defined, there is another opportunity to draw on any context analysis that has been carried out, and to think about how this relates to the outcome map in question. In its most pure form, risks and assumptions can be defined for each step of an outcome map or pathway.

However, for many people in public services, a light-touch version of this is more suitable, which brings in risks and assumptions across the pathway as a whole, defines and revises them, and reflects on them when conducting analysis. Risks and assumptions should help a non-specialist understand the real-world setting of the work represented in a map or pathway. It should help a reader see the logic behind the proposed activities and outcomes.

The art of outcome mapping

Outcome and impact mapping is not a precise and exacting tool that can be right or wrong; there are many ways in which outcome or impact maps and associated pathways might represent the work of a project, programme, organisation or partnership. Rather than discovering an objective truth, this is about balancing strategic priorities with practical incentives and being aware of the capacity of teams and organisations to work well with the maps and pathways as practical tools. As we emphasise throughout this book, this is a learning and improvement journey, and many iterations of outcome maps and pathways are usually required to get to a place where it is really working well.

Conclusions

This chapter has set out our approach to outcome or impact mapping as a tool for understanding the change that matters to an initiative. This really helps to get clarity on what is important about any approach and is usually an enjoyable way of reconnecting with the purpose of the work. As described in future chapters, outcome or impact maps can be tools for navigating complex change. Like geographical maps, they provide a sense of direction and purpose and keep everyone focused on the journey. We believe in outcome and impact maps as a framework for meaningful evaluation – to track, learn, reflect and report on the difference an initiative has made – as the next chapters show.

Try it yourself

If you want to try this approach to outcome or impact mapping for your own work, you can find a copy of our headings on the Matter of Focus website. (See the resources section in Chapter 11 for a link.)

You can set them along a desk or table, and use sticky notes to set out your initiative.

- If you have funders' outcomes, project outcomes or organisation aims that should be included, start with those.
- Separate the different processes – talk about who is engaged in the 'who with' column, and not 'what we do'. Separate learning outcomes from behaviour change outcomes. (Sometimes we even snip a funder's outcome in two if these are mixed up.)
- We often start with high-level outcomes, then activities, and then work out the story in the middle.
- It might take a bit of time to get this right!

To give you an idea of what this might look like, Figure 6.9 shows an example of a forest school running in the summer holidays.

Figure 6.9: An outcome map for a simple intervention (a children's forest school)

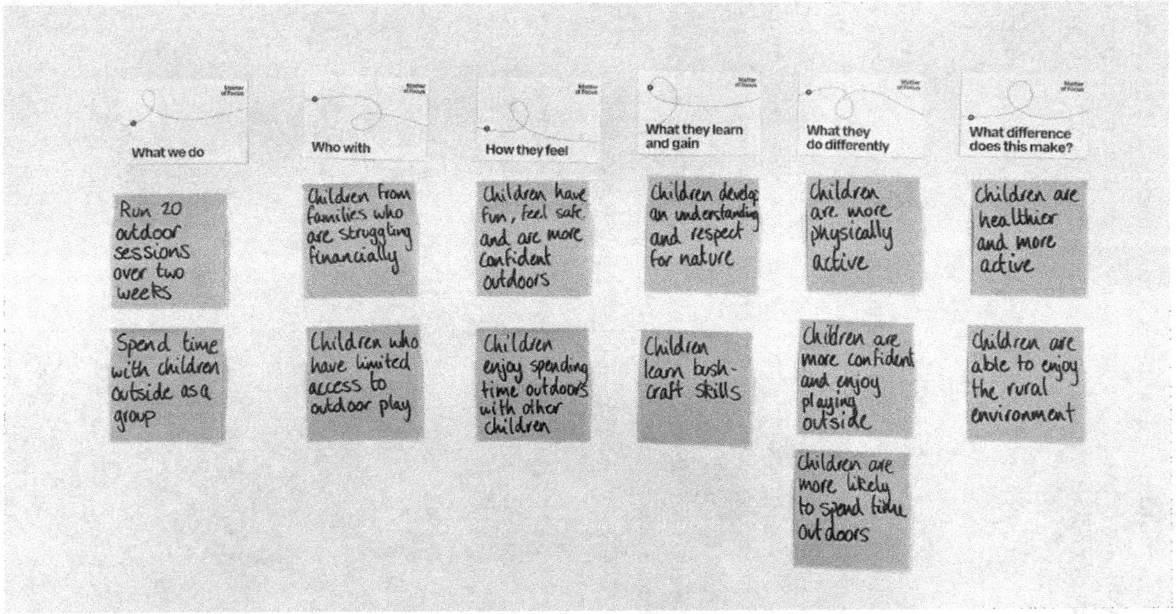

7

Get going on your data, evidence and feedback improvement journey

Wouldn't it be amazing to have all of the data and information at your fingertips to understand the change you want to see in the world? When so much data is available, and ways of collecting data have become more streamlined, it can be exasperating not to be able to pull together what is needed for the practical job of understanding whether something is making the difference intended.

We have already outlined why trying to understand complex work is difficult, and that using data is not a technical-rational process but rather a relational one – where the process of sense making together can be as important as the data, evidence or feedback you use.

In Chapter 3 we discussed challenges in the culture and in the ways of working with data for most organisations. We suggested the need to go on a data improvement journey. In this chapter we present some practical ways to approach the journey, and tools and techniques to help on the way.

This chapter covers:

- improving approaches to data, evidence and feedback;
- how to undertake a data audit;
- how to fill the gaps understanding;
- practical data collection techniques;
- feedback in action.

We will be using examples from some of our clients, including how a research body improved feedback, ways of building on reflective practice, and getting feedback fast.

We hope you will be able to use some of the ideas presented here and apply them to any setting, share them with colleagues and start on a data improvement journey. The message is the same as in Chapter 4 – just get going with your data improvement journey!

A quick reminder of what we mean when we talk about data, evidence and feedback:

Data: any quantitative, numerical or qualitative collected information about what an initiative is doing and what difference it makes.

Evidence: more formal and processed information such as evaluation reports (for the work in question or from other similar work) or the research evidence – for example, systematic reviews or research that relates to the themes of the work. 'Evidence' can also be used informally as a term to refer to all of the above.

Feedback: any formal or informally collected feedback that is being used (even just from informal discussions) to understand what is going on. This can include what people say directly about the work, feedback forms, pictures, reflections, or reflective practice.

Improving approaches to data, evidence and feedback

The first step to improving any approach to data, evidence and feedback is to be ruthlessly pragmatic. This means focusing on the usability of any data collection, addressing the capacity to work with data and feedback, and where possible to stop collecting evidence where there isn't a plan to use it. It's easy to be idealistic about the perfect survey, or the large data set that might be useful, but without a plan and the resources to gain insights from that data, then it really is a waste of time.

Being pragmatic can throw up some of the data culture challenges discussed in Chapter 3. If simple qualitative feedback would be the most useful thing in the time available, but the culture values randomised control trials, then it will be harder to make the case. It's sometimes necessary to be brave on the first steps on a data improvement journey, but eventually this will lead to being able to tell a strong evidence-informed story that will satisfy the sceptics. Getting to grips with your data, evidence and feedback often brings real practical benefits as well as being a critical step in knowing your work makes a difference.

Here are some of the things we have found help organisations on their data improvement journey.

Define the appropriate scale for data collection

Whether at the start of a project, or looking at work in progress, it can be helpful to think carefully about the appropriate scale of data for the initiative. Is it about monitoring, evaluating or testing an innovation? How many people are involved, and is it possible to get feedback from them? What capacity is there for bringing together and analysing data?

If the initiative is something that has been done many times, light-touch monitoring is probably adequate. If it's something new and untested, the focus might be on the least secure assumptions about the work. If there is the desire and capacity for an in-depth evaluation, a grander data collection plan would be appropriate.

What scale is the work on? Thinking about what is needed to understand if it is making a difference can be a good way of focusing on what data is needed. This will look quite different for a small community-led initiative and for a large-scale multipartner programme.

Focus on usability

Is the data going to be used, who will be involved and when will this happen? These usability questions can also help with the shape and scale of any evidence plans. Starting with this end in mind focuses efforts on what is most important to know and why. Many of our clients start with a focus on data about activities and engagement as these will be the cornerstones of their work. This could include thinking about whether delivery is going as planned, if engagement is as anticipated, and how people who are engaged react to getting involved with the work. Starting with that kind of data, reviewing and adapting, and then moving on to gathering data about learning or behaviour-change outcomes can be a pragmatic way forward.

We emphasise data collection, review, analysis and reporting cycles that embed learning in the work. Collecting and collating data in this way slowly builds up a contribution story. The next two chapters address analysis and reporting, but please keep these in mind as you read this chapter.

Mixed data is best

We made the case for using mixed data for understanding complex work in Chapter 3. It's not possible to understand the difference you are making with numbers alone. A patchwork quilt of data specifically tailored to the initiative in hand is most suitable for understanding complex change. Using a contribution analysis approach also embraces pragmatism by starting with the data you have, highlighting the gaps, and filling these. We call this a data audit, and we have taken many clients through this process.

How to undertake a data audit

When we work with organisations to help understand the difference they make, one of the things we usually do is a data audit. This is to help build a picture of the data, evidence and feedback an initiative has or can easily get. Even new initiatives are usually contained within organisations that have systems and processes in place before the work commences.

Step 1: What data already exists about the difference this makes?

A data audit process starts with the process of collating all of the current sources of data, evidence and feedback. This might include administrative data, spreadsheets, feedback forms, social media reports, photos, case studies, previous evaluations, research that supports the work, notes about people, notes from meetings, reflective practice records, standard feedback questions/methods.

Collating this list of potential sources of data, evidence and feedback can be a complex process, depending on the work and the size and scale of the ambition for impact tracking. For some organisations, this throws up questions about current record keeping and feedback practices that can take a while to unravel, but ultimately help to improve practice and processes.

Step 2: What does or doesn't your existing data tell you?

Thinking across the levels of outcomes in our outcome mapping approach and plotting out what existing data is available is the next step in the data audit process. We ask clients to set out their existing data against our headings (what we do, who with, and so on, as outlined in Chapter 6).

Setting out the current data like this helps to immediately understand where data is stronger and weaker, and what gaps need to be filled. It's usual to have plenty of evidence of delivery (what we do) and engagement (who with) but harder to evidence learning and behaviour-change outcomes as there are usually fewer data sources for higher level outcomes. Other questions that can help with this data audit process, are whether the data is in good shape, needs improvement, or perhaps it is possible to stop collecting some things.

Once this has been set out, then data can be mapped against specific outcome areas (see Figure 7.1). We start doing this with

Figure 7.1: Data audit on two columns of an outcome map

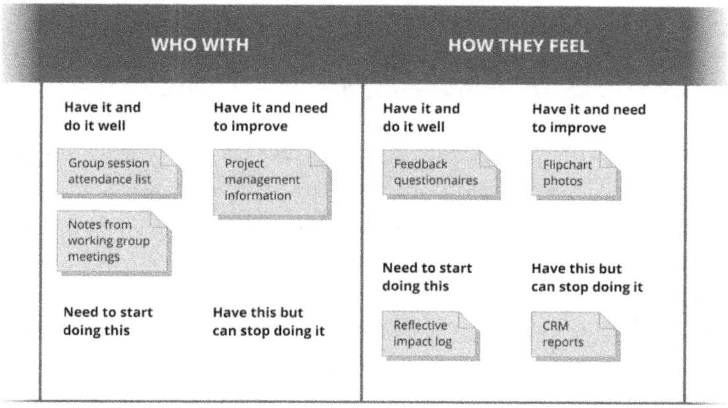

the outcome map headings, and then move to look at pathways (as outlined in Chapter 6).

Asking the question 'How will we know if this is progressing well?' for each part of the map creates a picture of where data sources can be used, and where new methods need to be developed. This helps to clarify exactly what feedback is needed for the gaps and to shape how they will be filled.

Step 3: What gaps in the data are there for each pathway?

The third step in the data audit process is to look at the specific pathways, and the stepping stones on each one. Is there data that can help evidence each one? What are the gaps? This then helps to identify where and when additional data might be needed.

How to fill gaps in understanding

Most initiatives will find it easier to explain and evidence what they do and who with than behaviour-change or final outcomes. Using the outcome map and pathways, as described above, can bring into sharp focus where further data is needed.

Radical pragmatism is the approach to remember! There is no point in creating lots of data sources right across a map without thinking about how, when and by whom the data will be collected and analysed. It is most efficient to use the same data source across different levels in a pathway – for example, one feedback form might find out how people feel, what they have learned or gained and what they are doing differently.

Outcome maps and pathways as data collection guides

The beauty of an outcome map pathway is that it becomes the guide for collecting and collating data, evidence and feedback. Figure 7.2 is an example from the fictional wellbeing service we introduced in Chapter 6. This is the 'what they do differently' column from the 'sharing the learning' pathway. The pathway shows that the changes envisaged are that 'practitioners, managers and planners make changes to improve their services', and that they 'deliver effective services and improve practice'.

Figure 7.2: Using a pathway as a framework for data collection

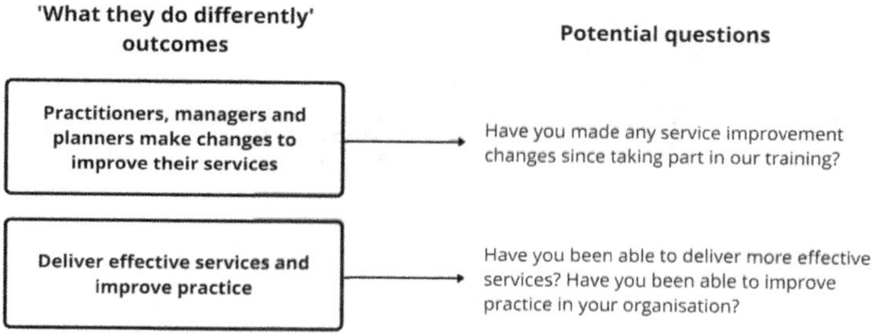

'What they do differently' outcomes

Potential questions

Practitioners, managers and planners make changes to improve their services

→ Have you made any service improvement changes since taking part in our training?

Deliver effective services and improve practice

→ Have you been able to deliver more effective services? Have you been able to improve practice in your organisation?

These items on the pathway help guide the sort of feedback questions that might be asked.

Figure 7.2 shows how the specific stepping stones in the pathway can be used to focus on the data needed. Once this data is collected, it is clear exactly how it can be used to evidence this part of the pathway to build the contribution story.

We developed the table in Figure 7.3 as a way of guiding people through the sorts of data that might be useful at different levels across an outcome map or pathway. This list is not prescriptive, rather it is intended as a way of thinking about potential data sources and methods.

Going through this data audit process is the first part of the data improvement journey. The second part is to collect additional data to fill the gaps.

Practical data collection techniques

Most of the organisations we support need to fill gaps in their understanding of what difference they make. These are some of the approaches we commonly suggest to help with this.

Formalise insights – reflective impact log

It's common to be so focused on data about the people engaged in an initiative that the great insights of the people delivering the work get overlooked. Often, people managing and supporting an initiative understand what has gone well, what has been

Figure 7.3: Different kinds of data across outcome levels

	What we do	Who with	How they feel	What they learn and gain	What they do differently	What difference does this make?
Feedback	Descriptions of what was delivered	Descriptions of who was engaged and why	Feedback from participants on their reaction to the activities	Feedback from participants about knowledge, skills, capacities or attitudes that have changed	Feedback from participants about changes in behaviour, policy or practice	Logical extrapolation from previous feedback or direct feedback from participants
Quantitative/ aggregated data	Number of activities	Graphs or other quantitative data on people engaged	Likert scales showing people's reactions	Likert scales on specific knowledge or skills gained	Likert scales on specific behaviour changes	Case studies of individuals, links to national or local data
Staff reflections about internal learning	Record of process and challenge and how they were tackled	Description of partnership/ partners	Reflections on process	Reflections from team on learning	Reflections from team on behaviour, policy or practice changes	Records from team of what has changed
Reflections about process and outcomes			Participant observation of reactions of participants	Participant observation of changes in knowledge, skills or attitude	Participant observation of any changes	
Visual data	Photos and videos of activities	Pictures of people involved (with consent)		Images of outputs from activities	Images of things that have changed	

challenging and where there has been the most impact. We developed a reflective impact log format that provides a framework to think through the different levels of impact in an outcome map. If people at the heart of a programme can collectively or individually record their insights systematically, they form a great source of evidence. People also enjoy this process, and it can help shape what other data is needed to test these reflections. For example, if someone supporting people observes and reflects on a change those people seem to be making, the next step would be to ask them directly and collect further evidence.

Reflective impact logs are useful because they:

- allow sharing of what went well and any challenges in the delivery of a programme or initiative;
- bring in early reflections before other data is available;
- help build up a full description of what was delivered and why;
- help shape and understand what other data will be needed to build a robust contribution story.

Links to our reflective impact log template can be found in the resources section of this book.

Bridging the gap between data about people and organisation-wide impact

One major challenge for organisations delivering services and support for people is how to bridge the gap between the rich data they have about individuals (usually in some kind of case notes) and the insights they need as organisations. It's easy to say how many people have been supported, but, as discussed throughout this book, those numbers can't tell the story of what difference the work makes. There might be rich stories in the case notes about how people have been supported or engaged, but it can be really frustrating trying to showcase these at an organisational level given the practical difficulty in aggregating them – let alone the ethics and confidentiality issues that need to be considered. Putting some kind of systematic reflection process into the mix can help with this issue.

Figure 7.4: From individual to organisational data

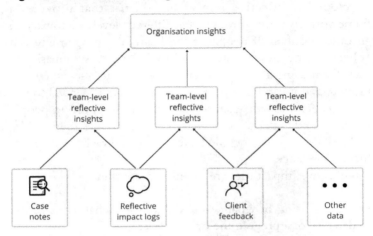

There are two main ways of doing this. The first is reflective practice sessions, where practitioners can record their thoughts in a reflective impact log, as explained in Figure 7.4, or on a flip chart through discussion, then taking a photo of the flip charts. The second is case note sampling.

Case note sampling

Case note sampling is a technique where a random sample of around 30 notes about individuals are sampled from case notes. A dedicated group then analyses these notes with a mindset of outcomes and impact. This highlights where the main contribution is, but also helps to improve recording practice as practitioners get to view one another's notes in detail and understand why it is important to have consistent recording principles. There is more about this analysis process in the next chapter.

Individual outcome recording

Finally, some of the organisations we work with record information on changes for outcomes for the people they support. There is a plethora of approaches to doing this, from using standardised tools, such as the Outcome Star, to capturing outcomes defined by individuals and progress towards this in individual case records. However, the most important factor when deciding what approach to take is to ensure it is meaningful to both the people benefiting from your support and those working with them. (See the Meaningful and Measurable report for a full discussion of these issues (Miller and Barrie, 2016).) Taking time to really understand how staff record outcomes is also critical, with good recording a cornerstone of good practice with people as well as generating vital evidence to understand changes in outcomes (Social Care Wales, 2022).

Getting feedback when it's difficult

If you're working in policy influencing or public engagement, there may be limited opportunities to formally collect data. As an example, it's inappropriate when giving evidence to a government committee to hand out a postcard asking for their thoughts! If there is limited time or contact with people, for example in museums and art galleries or public events, there are fewer opportunities for formal feedback. There are things that can be done (and some of the rapid feedback techniques below might help here), but one of the under-rated impact assessment tools is observation.

Whatever the setting, it is possible to sit down and formally record any observations, and if this is done as a team, it can be even more robust. A reflective impact log can work here, but it can be helpful even just to think through and record:

- what went well;
- what were the challenges;
- how people reacted;
- whether you got the engagement you hoped for;
- what you think might happen next.

As with the other reflective processes described here, this can also help identify opportunities to improve your data and shore up the observations. If the reflection was that people on the government committee reacted well to the input, and seemed engaged and interested, how might this be followed up? Maybe by looking at the record of the meeting, finding out what the next steps will be for the issue, and following through to the policy process. If the observations in a public space highlight the way people interact with it, maybe that is what further feedback can be collected on.

Rapid feedback techniques

Taking a pragmatic approach to data collection means making it as quick and simple as possible to collect and digest any feedback. It's not always appropriate to hand out a questionnaire or take people through a lot of questions about their experience. Of course, all of these techniques need to be tailored to the needs of the people taking part, including any specific communication or interaction needs, but here are some examples.

Quick feedback form

It can be helpful to break feedback collection into manageable chunks, and one way we do this is with a quick feedback form. Simple feedback about what was good about any input or activity and what could be improved can be very effective, and you can ask people about what they learned and what they might do differently (Figure 7.5).

Figure 7.5: Quick feedback form

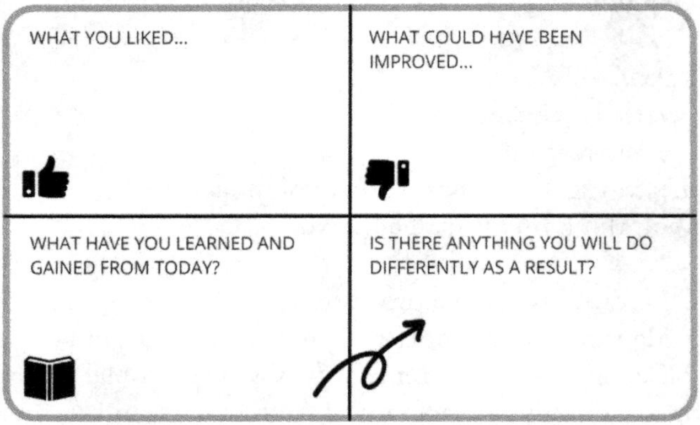

WHAT YOU LIKED...	WHAT COULD HAVE BEEN IMPROVED...
👍	👎
WHAT HAVE YOU LEARNED AND GAINED FROM TODAY?	IS THERE ANYTHING YOU WILL DO DIFFERENTLY AS A RESULT?

Figure 7.5 is plain and formal, but this can also be made much more informal – with icons of thumbs up and thumbs down for the top part, and 'what I learned', 'what I am going to do' in the bottom part. This form can be on paper, on a virtual whiteboard, on a postcard or on the wall. Some version of a positive and negative comment, of what people have learned or gained, and their intentions afterwards is useful in many settings.

Another way to use this quick feedback form is to include outcomes from a pathway in the questions. Our own map includes that people:

- feel our approach is in line with their values;
- learn about the importance of working with outcomes;
- feel more confident about working with data and evidence.

We collect responses to one of these three questions each time we ask for quick feedback on our activities, and circle round the questions over time to build up a picture of our progress.

This simple feedback approach is well suited to online events – the form can be used on a virtual whiteboard, or the questions can be asked in the meeting chat function.

Flip charts

If you were to look at our phones, you would find lots of photos of flip charts! Evidence collection doesn't always have to be formal, and it's great just to grab the meeting reflections, the themes or other useful information that has been recorded to keep as evidence.

Flip chart feedback is also good in group settings – asking people to add stickers to a Likert scale on paper, or to put down one word about how they feel, are quick and effective ways of generating evidence for an impact story.

Smiley faces

You probably feel it's crass being asked to tap a smiley or frowning face as you leave the bathroom at an airport, but this simple kind of feedback can also be really effective. It can be done electronically, on paper or in other ways. Figures 7.6 and 7.7, from a Brook advisory clinic in Bristol, show a very simple way

Figure 7.6: Simple feedback example from Brook

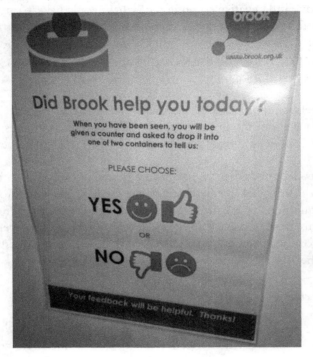

Figure 7.7: Simple feedback example from Brook (continued)

Figure 7.8: Simple feedback airport example

of getting rapid feedback as part of evaluation, by asking people to put a token in a thumbs-up or thumbs-down container.

It's even better if combined with qualitative feedback – see the following example from an airport, where the team are encouraging both a smiley face response and other feedback to help them understand if they are helping people through security well (Figure 7.8).

Images

With the right permissions, images of activities or of feedback can be a great record of impact, and a way of bringing an impact report to life. Images might illustrate activities or engagement and, occasionally, people doing something they wouldn't have done without the initiative.

Informal feedback or 'thank bank'

Informal feedback might include emails, tweets, pictures or cards. Many of our clients face the problem of how to capture this feedback so it can be used in a meaningful way.

We suggest collating these in an informal feedback record – some people like to call this a 'thank bank' although it can include negative as well as positive feedback. This means that this kind of informal feedback is all in one place and can be used as a source of evidence for impact and outcome tracking.

Our own informal feedback record is a simple Excel workbook, with two pages. The first is for informal feedback we get via email, social media and directly spoken to us. We record this, along with a quote where possible, and whether we have permission to use it publicly. The second page records the presentations we give, the numbers who came and a description. This helps to show our reach.

Our clients adapt their own version of this record to suit their context; some have a sheet for thank you letters, feedback from website pop-ups, or other sources where they get informal feedback. This is a very simple way of collating evidence and making it more formal. Of course, it is only as good as the information you add to it!

Do it your way

Finally, when thinking about how to collect feedback, it's important to do it your way – that is, to do it in a way that suits the setting, context and people involved. It can feel like quite a shift to go from a creative activity to filling in a form, or from a conversational interaction to formal feedback. Try to design the feedback collection methods in the style of the activity being delivered, and tailor them to the preferences of the people involved. That includes making them accessible for people with communication needs.

The most impressive version of this we have seen is with our client Starcatchers. They were running a programme of creative events for children with their kinship carers. During the programme, the families and artists developed a superhero theme and created superhero costumes for the children. To gather feedback from these families, the team set up the words 'agree' and 'disagree' on the wall at the end of the hall and asked families to zoom their superhero children, on skateboards, to the wall to reflect their answers to some questions. These included 'We have enjoyed taking part' and 'We have more ideas of how to be creative at home together'.

Feedback in action

Health Technology Wales: web interface feedback loop

Health Technology Wales is a national body tasked with reviewing health technologies and sharing their findings with the health and social care sectors and government in Wales. They added a simple feedback pop-up box to find out more about people downloading their advice and guidance from their website (Figure 7.9). Although many people skip this step, they quickly got over 100 responses that helped them understand their impact. They also ask people if they are happy to be followed up, creating an extra channel for further feedback. This method is especially useful for information sharing, where what people do and whether it makes a difference is beyond the control of the project.

Scottish Social Services Council: reflective impact log

The reflective impact log is one of the most popular tools we use in our work and was co-designed with Workforce Development team members from the Scottish Social Services Council during the course of our evaluation work with them. Like many of the organisations we work with, their work was very varied and often carried out in partnership with other agencies.

While they were easily able to capture feedback on the impact of some of the activities they carried out, for example delivering training, it was much harder to get feedback on

Figure 7.9: Information sharing feedback pop-up, Health Technology Wales

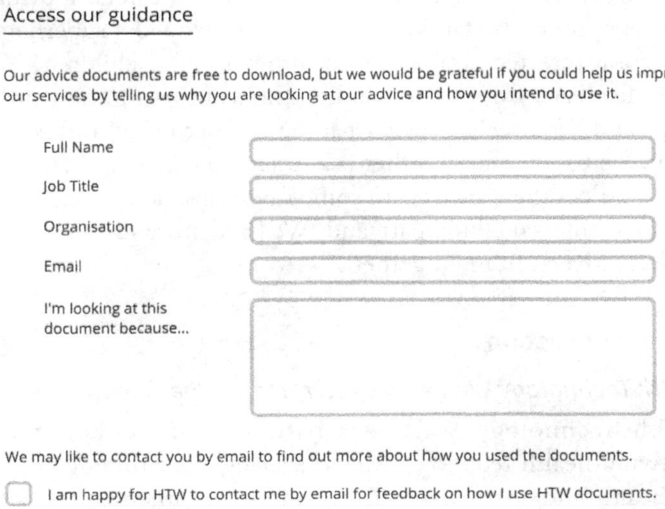

Access our guidance

Our advice documents are free to download, but we would be grateful if you could help us improve our services by telling us why you are looking at our advice and how you intend to use it.

Full Name

Job Title

Organisation

Email

I'm looking at this document because...

We may like to contact you by email to find out more about how you used the documents.

☐ I am happy for HTW to contact me by email for feedback on how I use HTW documents.

the impact of their policy work, which was often carried out over long periods of time and involved multiple meetings and points of contact. They were, however, able to tell a clear story from their point of view of how this work was shaping policy. We agreed to build on their existing ethos of reflective practice and develop a tool that they could use together and individually to systematically reflect over time on the impact of their policy work.

We used this tool in a range of ways during our work together:

- as part of an action learning set to reflect on the difference team members participation had made;
- to individually reflect on progress through a policy influencing process;
- to capture the impact of events.

East Renfrewshire peer support project: case note audit

East Renfrewshire Health and Social Care Partnership (HSCP) commissioned the voluntary sector provider Penumbra to deliver a Peer Support Service for people recovering from mental health difficulties or harmful alcohol and/or drug use, with a view to embedding peer approaches into the Partnership. Towards the end of their project evaluation we developed a process of case note review. We did this to try to get a better sense of the experiences of people who had finished their time with the service and to supplement the data we had previously collected about people who were actively using the service. Peer workers selected a sample of case notes and reviewed them using a data collection form which was based on their outcome map headings and on the stepping stones under each heading. For example, the following question explored what people had learned and gained:

> Please say a bit about how your perception of the person you were working with gained as a result of your interactions. Have they changed their perspective on anything since joining the service? You may feel the agreed outcomes (below) do not cover what you perceived to be happening, so don't feel limited by them.

Agreed outcomes for the 'what they learn and gain' column:

- People using the service know what matters to them and how peer support can help.
- Hope for the future, a better understanding of recovery and a belief that recovery is possible.
- Confidence in oneself and in the Peer Support Service.
- The HSCP gains greater understanding of peer support and how it complements other services.

About Dementia: fast feedback

The About Dementia programme team is based in Age Scotland and has been funded by the Life Changes Trust to enable activists with dementia to shape policy and practice. A key part of the team's work is running events and workshops, bringing together activists who are living with dementia and unpaid carers with professionals to transform policy and practice.

Since the beginning of their project, the About Dementia team have used our quick feedback form to get responses from everyone attending their events. This has been important in reassuring them that most attendees have found the events valuable and believe in what About Dementia is doing. Some of the forms have identified areas for improvement, which the team have been able to act on.

Conclusion

Throughout this book we have highlighted that using data, evidence and feedback is a complex process, and not one that can be quickly and easily 'applied'. This chapter has set out ways to think and orientate any organisation or initiative to the data it needs to understand the difference it makes. There are a lot of ideas here, and no one organisation will immediately use them all. Thinking about this as a data improvement journey and starting out by trying to improve, learning about how that helps the work and affects capacity, and then taking the next step is the pragmatic way of getting to a better place.

Try it yourself

At your next team meeting, spend some time reflecting on your impact. If you have an outcome map, then use it as a way of reflecting.

Record what people say, but also pay attention to the conversation. What are you learning? How might you get extra evidence to substantiate what people think is happening in the initiative?

If you like, use our reflective impact log process. (See the Resources chapter for a link.)

8

Tracking progress towards outcomes and impacts

So far, we have shared some helpful tools for developing a clear understanding of the outcomes and impacts that matter to any initiative, expressed in an outcome map with risks and assumptions. We have considered how this lends itself to understanding data, evidence and the feedback needed to improve learning and delivery. You may even have some ideas about how to gather more helpful data in creative ways. The next step is to start thinking about how to assess whether your work is making a difference.

As already highlighted in Chapter 4, we're not fans of simplistic approaches to assessing outcomes as met or unmet. Instead, we believe that the journey to improving outcomes or maximising impacts is never over. Effective organisations that own their outcomes are always seeking to improve, reflect and learn, to align resources and develop systems and processes to make the best contribution possible. Taking time to systematically analyse and assess progress is a linchpin of this approach. In this chapter we will outline what is required to analyse, assess and track progress towards outcomes or impacts ahead of reporting, and share some simple and accessible ways of thinking that can help even people with no experience of analysis get going.

This chapter covers:

• getting started with data analysis;
• a practical framework for assessing and tracking the difference you make;
• three levels to help shape analysis.

Analysis need not be a scary or specialist process. It is something that we all do every day. The key to getting going with analysing and assessing progress is to harness these everyday sense-making skills that are so important when working with complex initiatives. We hope that this chapter will give you the confidence to do this.

Getting started with data analysis

We believe in the power of starting with the end in mind and having a clear sense of what success looks like for any process. This is the foundation for being able to break a process down and plan for that success. Many of the organisations we work with lack a clear sense of what good analysis looks like and what they need in order to do it. They often have experience, systems and processes for articulating outcomes and impacts, and for gathering data and reporting, but when it comes to analysis, especially of qualitative data, they don't know where to start.

Public service organisations often don't have the right tools to support their analysis. There are some very powerful tools on the market that support qualitative and quantitative analysis, but they are primarily aimed at researchers and not well suited to the more pragmatic analytical approaches that public service organisations need. We have developed our approach and tools with this gap in mind. We believe that with the right scaffolding and support, people can bring together different sources of data effectively to assess and track progress towards outcomes and demonstrate impact.

But first let's be clear what we mean by analysis.

What is data analysis?

The term analysis usually describes a process of looking at a body of data and information and extracting some meaning. Across public services, people use a range of analytical approaches. In many contexts, most analysis is carried out on quantitative data. At its simplest, quantitative analysis involves answering questions using numerical data to generate understanding of trends or patterns. Sometimes data may be subject to statistical analysis to generate insights that can be applied more widely.

Having a basic knowledge of quantitative analytical techniques is important for knowing your work is making a difference. It's helpful to be able to work with numerical data to track the number of people who have engaged with an initiative, to be able to understand percentages and frequencies and trends in responses to feedback, for example.

Qualitative analysis is the process of reviewing a body of data and information and pulling out key trends or messages from that data. Qualitative analysis approaches can be used to analyse data of all types: text, images, numbers, sounds and observations.

Qualitative analysis is a skill most people use all the time. If you're in a new place and wondering what restaurant to eat at, you might read reviews, menus, look at price information, look in the window of a few restaurants, and then make a decision about which restaurant is going to meet your needs. The same process of reviewing a range of different sources of data and evidence, and using critical thinking, applies to understanding the difference an initiative makes.

The process of qualitative analysis

There are a few considerations for this process of qualitative analysis. We have separated these into questions, preliminary analysis and developing analysis.

Questions

We always recommend starting a process of qualitative analysis by clarifying the questions that need to be asked of that data. When using our approach, the outcome map generates those questions (see Chapter 7). Each item on an outcome map (each 'stepping stone') presents something that it is important to know from the data. For example, in the 'how they feel' column, there might be a stepping stone saying 'included', because the initiative needs to make sure people feel included. It would then be worth collecting and analysing data on whether people felt included.

Knowing what questions you want to ask helps to engage in a practical and achievable process of qualitative analysis without getting too lost in the data. In contrast, a popular approach to qualitative analysis, called grounded theory, recommends starting the analysis process not with questions but with an open-minded review of the data, allowing the questions to emerge from the data rather than the other way around. This kind of deep and time-consuming approach might be appropriate for academic researchers, but is not required for pragmatic analysis of progress towards outcomes in public service settings.

Preliminary analysis

The next step in the analysis process is to review all the data and evidence that relate to those questions or – if there is an outcome map – the particular stepping stone or step in focus. Making notes and bullet points as thoughts emerge is a good starting point. Questions like: what kinds of things are people learning from this initiative? What are they saying about the activities that have been most significant in shaping their learning?

Developing analysis

Having carried out a preliminary analysis of any data and identified themes, the next step is to review documents again and look for evidence to support, test or further develop the analysis. This is a good stage to move from bullet points and notes to a more coherent narrative and to consider if there is any broader evidence you might draw on to support what you are seeing in the data. It is also a good time to go back to your risks and assumptions and look at what your data can tell you about how they have played out in practice.

Starting to write up your analysis early is key, refining and improving it as your understanding deepens and in response to new data. Throughout this phase of analysis, it is really helpful to talk to others and check out your interpretations of the data.

With the Life Changes Trust, we used an outcome map as a tool to collectively analyse data with young people who were advisors to the Trust. In a virtual meeting during COVID restrictions, we were able to consider the data emerging around specific parts of the outcome map and work together to rate these and include the advisors' perspectives in the narrative.

Maximising rigour

If you're new to qualitative analysis, you might be reading this process and wondering, how will I know if I'm right? What about bias? What if I see something different in the data from my colleagues? These are important questions. Qualitative analysis approaches recognise that everybody brings themselves to the analysis process and may interpret the same data in slightly different ways.

To address this, it can be helpful to conceptualise data analysis as lying on a continuum. Some data can be taken at face value (such as the number of people who came to a training session) while others need much more interpretation (such as what they say they learned during the training). A robust qualitative analysis process involves thinking carefully about the data and reflecting on the factors that might have influenced them. For example, feedback on a service will be shaped by the questions asked, the mood of the person giving the feedback, their understanding of what will happen to their feedback and how it might influence their service going forward. Reflecting and accounting for these influences on the data is critical to taking a robust approach.

Adopting a transparent and replicable process to carrying out analysis is also key to rigour. Qualitative approaches to analysis explicitly recognise that different people may reach slightly different conclusions or tell a different story from the same body of data; however, it should be possible to unpack the key parts of the process undertaken. What was the data analysed? What questions were asked of that data? Who was involved? What was the time frame for the analysis? Building transparency into the analysis process ensures the findings are credible and that others are able to understand the conclusions reached. We do this using our outcome mapping approach as set out in the next section of this chapter.

A practical framework for assessing and tracking the difference you make

Over the past five years we have been refining our approach to support organisations to carry out analysis. We have aimed to make this as practicable and as robust as possible.

A process for analysing data, evidence and feedback

As already highlighted, analysis is an iterative process that organisations will go through many times, but it can be broadly broken down into a process with six parts.

Quick revision

In this section we refer to different parts of an outcome or impact map as follows:

Step – these are the different levels of outcomes and impacts in our approach: what we do, who with, how they feel, what they learn and gain, what they do differently, and what difference does this make.
Stepping stone – these are the specific items that make up any outcome or impact map and will be specific to the initiative in hand. These sit across the 'Step' levels, as illustrated in Figure 8.1.

Figure 8.1: Illustration of steps and stepping stones in an outcome map pathway

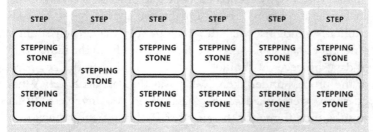

1. **Identify the right unit of analysis.** One of the biggest barriers people face to getting going with analysis is that they don't know where to start. We recommend breaking the analysis process down into the smallest meaningful units possible and going through these in turn. Within our approach, analysis takes place at step or stepping stone level.
2. **Assemble the relevant data and evidence.** Next, bring together all of the data and evidence that relate to the unit of analysis. Sometimes a source of evidence (such as survey results or notes from a meeting) will apply across different outcome levels; other times, to just one specific area – as described in Chapter 7.
3. **Clarify the questions.** Being crystal clear about the purpose of the analysis is the easiest way to save time. Most public service organisations have lots of rich data but don't have the capacity to extract all of the meaning and learning. It's more realistic to approach each item of data and evidence with a clear set of questions. In our approach, the step and stepping stone headings can easily be translated into questions – taking specific items from the outcome map or asking the broader questions of 'how did people feel?', 'what did they learn and gain?', and so on. We advocate a process of bringing together the level of outcome (in our approach, this means outcome levels like 'what they learn and gain') with the specific outcome on the map, and the evidence needed to understand progress – and then thinking about what questions are needed to understand progress. We call these 'success criteria'.
4. **Review the evidence in light of the questions.** This part of the process is as simple as reading through every evidence source and noting down any insights that connect to the questions. Capturing and sharing these early notes is important for engaging others in the analysis process.
5. **Draft and discuss preliminary analysis.** Having reviewed all of the relevant evidence sources, it's time to draft an initial assessment of progress. Again, this need not be perfectly polished, just enough information to allow others to review and give feedback. It can be beneficial at this stage to include reflections on the implications of this analysis for the work.

6. Agreeing and writing up findings. It is only once all of the previous steps have happened that it is possible to confidently write up the findings, illustrating them with visuals and quotes where appropriate. There is more guidance on how to do this in Chapter 9.

A holistic view of progress

Going through this process for specific outcomes at different levels enables an overarching contribution story for each aspect of an initiative's work to be built. It's important to assess progress and undertake analysis at both a step-by-step (or stepping stone) level and across a pathway. This is because your assessment of what happens at each step has to be informed by the step before. For example, if there is good evidence that the people that are important to an initiative have learnt new things and that they engaged well with the activities, then it is easier to build confidence about the contribution of the initiative to that new knowledge. However, if the evidence suggests that engagement with the initiative was poor, consider whether the new learning may have been influenced by other factors beyond the project, such as other training.

This process of assessing progress need not be taxing or overcomplicated. Instead, what is required is a systematic process of asking sensible questions and reflecting on answers in line with the evidence. It does take time, but not necessarily specialist skills. It is, however, something that people find improves with practice. By carrying out this kind of analysis regularly, a contribution story can be built up bit by bit.

Visualising progress and confidence in evidence

Working through this process generates a rich contribution story that is invaluable for those in the thick of working towards a specific change. However, there will be many who need to quickly understand the progress of the initiative who do not have time to read a lengthy report. This is a key challenge for qualitative approaches more generally, as they don't lend themselves to quick visual summaries in the way traditional quantitative approaches do.

We suggest making two judgements on any stepping stone within a pathway. The first is what the evidence tells you about the progress; the second is about confidence in the evidence. We like to encapsulate these ratings by illustrating the outcome map using different colours (for example, green for good progress and red for no progress). We add a second rating of a judgement of the strength of evidence, usually represented by the density of the colour. Together these ratings give a visual summary of the progress. Suggested criteria to underpin these assessments are summarised in Tables 8.1 and 8.2.

These two assessments are not set in stone, rather they help focus people's efforts on two things: first, where things are going well, and where there needs to be improvement, and second, where data is stronger or weaker, which allows for effort to be put into data collection where needed.

While this assessment of progress is most robust when carried out at the end of the analysis process, it can be effective in sparking discussion and supporting teams to get going with analysis.

In this section we have outlined an overall approach to analysing progress towards outcomes or impacts; however, in practice, there are many micro decisions to be made. In the following section we look at three different levels of analysis that

Table 8.1: Suggested criteria for progress towards outcomes or impacts

Progress assessment	Criteria
Great progress	• Enough people and groups will experience this in the timescale appropriate to the project • Risks have been mitigated and assumptions achieved
Some progress	• Some people and groups experience this in the timescale appropriate to the project • Some risks have been mitigated and some assumptions achieved
No progress	• Not enough people and groups experience this in the timescale appropriate to the project • Risks have not been mitigated and some assumptions have been found to be unrealistic

Table 8.2: Suggested criteria for confidence in data

Confidence assessment	Criteria
Very confident	**Most of these criteria apply** • More than one source of evidence with appropriate balance of types • Evidence collected purposefully and for this purpose • Reasonable number of responses • No disagreement between evidence sources • Backed up by other research • Analysis is clear and purposeful (someone else could replicate and get broadly the same results)
Some confidence	**Some of these criteria apply** • More than one evidence source with appropriate balance of types of evidence • Evidence is collected purposefully and for this purpose • Reasonable number of responses • No disagreement between sources • Backed up by other research • Analysis is clear and purposeful (someone else could replicate and get broadly the same results) **And/or** • There is some disagreement or lack of clarity in the findings • The data is mostly gathered opportunistically
Little confidence	**Few of the above criteria apply AND/OR** • There is disagreement within the data • Assessments are based solely on an individual's perspective

organisations need to progress through to reach a robust analysis of the progress of their work.

Three levels to help shape analysis

When seeking to understand the difference their work makes, we recommend that teams go through three levels of analysis, asking the following questions in turn:

1. Can this initiative make the difference it hopes to?
2. How does this initiative work: what helps and what gets in the way?
3. To what extent does this initiative make a difference?

More established teams with strong data might move through these levels of analysis quickly, while new initiatives might spend a couple of years on the first question. We run through what is involved at each level of analysis below.

Level 1: Can this initiative make the difference it hopes to?

If the imperative is to make sure that the initiative makes the best difference it can, this first question is the most important, and especially for new, innovative or untested ways of working. Teams that can answer this question positively can move forward with confidence in their approach. If not, it is a sharp reminder to stop and try something new. Answering this question also ensures that your evaluation efforts are built on a strong foundation and that the theory of change expressed in your outcome map pathway and risks and assumptions is a realistic reflection of how change happens.

When evidencing whether an initiative *can* make a difference, the most important sources of evidence are generally qualitative. This is the point in the analysis process where reviewing case studies, stories from practice and staff reflections can generate the insights required to know:

- Are the activities working as expected? Was it possible to deliver in the ways envisaged?
- Does the work get the engagement needed from at least some of the intended audience in the time frames allowed?
- Are people responding positively to the work, in enough cases?
- Is there any evidence that people who have been engaged learnt or gained new things as outlined in the pathway and outcome map?
- Are there any examples of people doing things differently, or policies and practices changing, informed by the initiative?
- Is there evidence of any difference made from the work for any of the people or organisations engaged?

This process sometimes highlights the need to change the theory of change, as expressed in the outcome map pathway, or the evidence-gathering practices.

When Edinburgh Long Term Conditions Programme went through this process, they realised that, while engaging unpaid carers was key to their theory of change, they had no evidence of this engagement. Digging deeper into their data, it became clear that there was no place to record any engagement that did happen. This initial round of analysis led to the service integrating a new section in their recording to explicitly capture engagement of unpaid carers. This, in turn, encouraged practitioners to really value and focus on this aspect of their work.

Level 2: How does this initiative work: what helps and what gets in the way?

This second level of analysis prompts engagement with the evidence about how an initiative is working across lots of people and places. This widens the focus of inquiry to where it's working well and where it isn't working. Careful analysis of context (see Chapter 5) and having articulated risks and assumptions are important foundations for this process. This level of analysis stress-tests the theory of change and generates clear written assumptions. It also produces information for understanding the limits of the initiative, which is vital for scaling up and spreading new approaches.

Engaging in analysis at this level requires organisations to broaden the data and evidence under consideration. This might include routinely collected data, feedback and reflective data. This data is used to consider the following questions for each step or stepping stone in a pathway or outcome map.

1. What progress has there been? What has already been realised and what has not been achieved yet? Where has there been variation in progress and are there any patterns in where the work has been more or less successful?
2. What are the factors that have helped this process? Are they consistent across people/contexts? Are they reflected in the assumptions?
3. What factors are getting in the way of progress? Are they consistent? Are they reflected in the risks?
4. How risky are the risks? Could they threaten progress? What, if anything, can be done in response?

This level of analysis can be the most time consuming but is where the richest insights for improvement often emerge. Once this analysis has been done, it doesn't need to be repeated, but instead assessments reviewed and updated over time.

Level 3: To what extent does this initiative make a difference?

It's common to ask this question first, because it is often the only question that funders or commissioners ask for information about. As we have already argued, this is not a question that can be answered by simply counting activities or outcomes and drawing a straight line between them. However, it is possible to answer this question with the right foundation in place, bringing together qualitative and quantitative data to evidence the extent of progress alongside a strong story of compelling and meaningful change. Teams that are confidently able to report at this level have reached high maturity in terms of owning their outcomes – with a robust theory of change, a streamlined approach to gathering qualitative and quantitative data, and good analysis systems in place.

Table 8.3 shows an example of the balance of qualitative and quantitative data required to evidence the extent to which a person-centred service improves outcomes for people.

While this level of analysis is about 'extent' of contribution to outcomes or impacts, it is worth recognising that the claims made about extent of impact are just that. For all the reasons outlined so far in this book, when working with complex change, there are always limits to numerical reporting and measures. A successful approach balances meaning with measurement and ensures that any data gathered, qualitative or quantitative, support good practice and are meaningfully analysed.

Table 8.3: Example qualitative and quantitative data for person-centred service across outcomes

Step	Qualitative	Quantitative
What we do	Description of what you do and why. Are you delivering well?	Numbers of activities run/staff involved/hours delivered.
Who with	Describe intended audience. Are you reaching them?	Number of people engaged per engagement plan. Demographic information.
How they feel	Summary of feedback, and reflections. Often includes the journey to a positive response.	For example, percentage of people who reported feeling safe and included.
What they learn and gain	Description of benefits. Quotes and summary of feedback.	For example, percentage of people who gained new skills.
What they do differently	Description of changes people are making.	Numbers of people making changes, for example accessing new support.
What difference does this make?	Feedback and reflections on how life is better.	Outcome measures, for example Outcome Star or WEMWBS.

Conclusion

It's critical to take the time to track progress towards outcomes or impacts to be able to tell a strong story of the contribution of any initiative to outcomes or impacts and to make the best contribution possible. We hope that this chapter has demonstrated that this is something anyone can do – no PhDs are required. It does necessitate investment of time and careful thinking, and it can be one of the hardest parts of building a strong contribution story. The benefits, however, are tremendous as, once invested, it is possible to start to tell an evidenced story of the difference any initiative makes. There are wider benefits too – streamlining effort on what matters in any setting, improving processes and practices, and having the time to sense make together as a team. All of these will help to make sure that the work is focused on the best difference it can make, and equip those doing the work with the tools and thinking they need to do that.

Try it yourself

One way of getting going with this is to draft some initial analysis, and then share it more widely. It doesn't matter how basic that analysis is – it can be in notes and bullet points – this process will help refine and improve it.

1. Share the analysis for a whole pathway or one or two steps, and give the team members time to read and digest (this can be before or during the session).
2. Mark out a flip chart or virtual whiteboard into four quadrants, each with a question:
   a. Do these findings resonate with you?
   b. Is there anything surprising?
   c. Is there anything you disagree with?
   d. Is there anything missing?
3. Ask your colleagues to discuss these questions in turn. If you are working online, using a virtual whiteboard can make the process really interactive and engaging.
4. These insights can be integrated into your analysis as you develop the next draft.

Doing this process over time will help you to develop and articulate what the data is telling you, and improve the data where needed.

9

Telling the story of the difference your work makes

Building a strong contribution story that explains and can evidence the difference your work makes to people, policy, practice or communities is not an easy task. Teams and organisations tell us how challenging it is to report on what difference their work has made and there is often a gap between the valuable work they do and the story they're able to tell about it. This is compounded because there are probably multiple stories they want to tell, to and with different people, for different purposes. Many organisations are great at explaining the richness of the work they do to support, empower or inspire people, but find it harder to link that to what difference it has made. Of course, our outcome mapping and tracking approach really helps to frame the process and make those links between activities and outcomes or impacts.

In this chapter we bring together our learning from working with many organisations and clients, as well as our own work in outcome and impact reporting. Thinking and using the language of 'contribution' – that is what contribution an initiative makes – can help make claims about this much clearer and stronger.

This chapter will consider:

- reporting in an outcome and impact-focused way;
- reporting for different audiences and purposes;
- using an outcome map as a framework for reporting;

- practical tips for great reporting;
- taking reporting forward.

We hope by reading this chapter you will understand how outcome-focused reporting can help you highlight the difference your work makes. This is the final part of the process we have described in Chapters 5 to 8, and a crucial one in making the case for your work. This chapter also aims to help think about different kinds of reporting for different purposes: reporting as a learning and improvement tool, as well as for sharing more widely.

Reporting in an outcome- and impact-focused way

There are many benefits of reporting in an outcome- and impact-focused way. While there is a lot of interest in the things that organisations do, it's only possible to understand their importance if the question of what difference they made is also clearly part of the story.

Focusing on outcomes and impacts makes a compelling and evidence-based case for the work and how it makes a difference to people. Following the processes in this book creates the building blocks for this strong contribution story – by plotting and tracking outcomes, using evidence effectively and learning as you go.

If the work is simple, or it's easy to demonstrate the difference made through numbers, then this kind of outcome-focused reporting isn't necessary. As with all of the approaches set out in this book, outcome-based reporting is really important where:

- there is a need to highlight *how* the work made a difference and *what* difference it made (process and outcome);
- change is complex and people-based;
- organisations or the authorising environment place an emphasis on outcomes or impact;
- numbers alone can't tell the story.

In some environments it is necessary to make the case for reporting like this to shine a light on what is important about work in complex settings, where cause and effect is harder to understand. When change is focused on people, then it can feel invisible, even when there is wonderful careful work to engage people and make a difference to their lives. By demonstrating *how* change happens – through an outcome map with analysis and evidence, pulled into a report – funders, boards, partners and wider stakeholders can see much more clearly what is important about the work, and why it matters to undertake careful and tailored approaches with people and communities.

Reporting is the part of the outcome and impact evaluation journey that lets other people understand the nuance of this work, and be able to support, promote and fund it.

The best outcome-focused reports:

- **focus on outcomes and impacts** – not just what was delivered, but also how it made a difference for people and communities;
- **link activities to outcomes and impacts** – clearly demonstrate how the specific activities are linked to the outcomes and impacts that matter;
- **are transparent** – use evidence well to show how conclusions have been reached, what data has been used and what that data relates to;
- **talk about the wider context** – show how the context has influenced the delivery of activities and outcomes;
- **illustrate findings** – with photographs, quotes, graphs and other visualisations.

These components have been discussed in other chapters in this book. The approach outlined – using outcome tracking – sets out the outcomes and impacts that matter and links activities to these through an outcome map, as described in Chapter 6. Chapters 7 and 8 laid out how to track outcomes by collecting and analysing data and evidence across an outcome map.

Chapter 5 shared approaches and tools for analysing the wider context and bringing this analysis into an outcome map by setting out risks and assumptions. Good outcome-focused reports will highlight some of this work – establishing the context for delivery and including analysis of the risks and assumptions in a contribution story.

A later section of this chapter looks at illustrating findings and picks up on some of the themes from the analysis discussion in Chapter 8.

Reporting for different audiences and purposes

Any communication specialist will tell you that reports should be aimed squarely at the intended audience, with a clear aim in mind, and that is no different for this kind of reporting. There is an added layer too, because reports might be serving different functions. Indeed, we encourage people using this approach to use reporting for learning as a first step to building a contribution story that might be shared more widely later. Carefully considering the audience and purpose can help shape what kind of analysis, narrative and illustrations are needed.

Reporting for internal learning

Once an outcome map and pathways have been established and data is being collected and analysed, then internal reporting for learning will help understand if the initiative is rolling out as intended, and if the evaluation framework and data collection plans are working well. This type of report might just be for the team conducting the evaluation work to review, it might be shared with colleagues, or it might be for an internal committee or board in the spirit of learning. Analysis can be tentative for this kind of reporting and could even be in note format. As described in Chapter 8, assessing progress and confidence in data can help focus on what is important and where data and evidence need to be improved. This is illustrated below for the fictional wellbeing service we have been using as an example throughout.

Figure 9.1 shows how progress ratings draw attention to stepping stones where progress is none or some, and to where there is less confidence in the data. This diagram helps focus on where there needs to be more effort to improve the initiative

Figure 9.1: Rating progress and confidence in evidence

Support people to improve wellbeing
Pathway progress

WHAT WE DO	WHO WITH	HOW THEY FEEL	WHAT THEY LEARN AND GAIN	WHAT THEY DO DIFFERENTLY	WHAT DIFFERENCE DOES THIS MAKE?
Have good conversations with people about factors impacting on their wellbeing and what they can do to change Progress: Great Confidence: High	People experiencing poor health and wellbeing Progress: Great Confidence: Some	This is a good conversation and I feel ready to make a change Progress: Great Confidence: Some	People know what matters to them and have the knowledge, confidence, skills to change Progress: Great Confidence: High	People make changes and actively manage their wellbeing Progress: Great Confidence: Some	People have improved wellbeing Progress: Some Confidence: Low
We run group sessions Progress: Great Confidence: High		This is for me Progress: Some Confidence: Some	Access to a range of relevant community supports and services Progress: Great Confidence: Low	People access supports from appropriate agencies Progress: No Confidence: Some	Services are used more appropriately Progress: Some Confidence: Low

(that is, where there is good evidence of not enough progress) and where effort should be on better data (for example, weak evidence of strong progress needs further testing to ensure that progress really is good). For learning purposes, this view of what is happening can really help stay on track.

Reporting for improvement

This is quite often the next step on a reporting journey. Reporting for improvement is usually for an internal audience and concentrates on what early data collection is highlighting about whether the initiative is progressing as envisaged, what is going well, where the challenges are, and how risks and assumptions are playing out. Reporting in this way allows teams and organisations to change elements of the approach that don't seem to be working, amplify those that do, and redesign if needed. In some cases, this will include using improvement methodology data collection approaches as part of outcome tracking.

Reporting for accountability

Outcome- and impact-focused reporting can help to contextualise and widen accountability requirements. Including key performance indicators or required data points in a mixed qualitative and numerically evidenced report can help place performance data within a richer contribution story. When reporting for accountability purposes, a more robustly analysed outcome map would be expected, with illustrations where appropriate.

Reporting for raising awareness and communication

Outcome- and impact-focused reports really lend themselves to the job of reporting more widely on an initiative and how it has made a difference, but again require a more polished narrative with illustrations. Here, case studies become useful (and will be discussed later in this chapter), as well as quotes from people highlighting what difference has been made.

Often, communications and marketing professionals within organisations can help, although it is essential not to overclaim.

Reporting to funders

The requirements of different funders are varied, but an outcome- or impact-focused report helps funders see how their money has been used to make a difference. Some funders are open to learning and improvement type reports in the early stages of an initiative. If a funder has commissioned work on outcomes or included outcomes in their reporting requirements, then it is essential these are included in the outcome map and pathways so that any reporting matches these requirements – there is no point in having both an outcome-tracked report and then another report for the funder. Ideally, bringing these together means that it is possible to demonstrate that the work has met the funder's requirements, while also showing how it made a difference, and elaborating on these requirements through rich qualitative data that supplement any measures.

Using an outcome map as a framework for reporting

Outcome mapping and tracking means that an outcome map and pathways are the foundations for reporting. Using the framework of 'what we do', 'who with', and so on, reports have to move up the outcome levels, and end with 'what difference does this make?'

We have found this framework useful as a basis for reporting, summarising and creating case studies. They work well for the following reasons.

Outcome maps and pathways link activities and outcomes

Using the outcome map, pathway or other theory of change approaches creates clear and logical links between what was delivered and what difference it makes. It immediately moves the story beyond what an initiative has done and towards outcomes and impacts. The 'so what?' question has to be answered if a report is based on outcome mapping and tracking.

In traditional models of evaluation, activities are often referred to as 'outputs', but we like to think about 'what we did' in a broad way that might cover what was delivered (outputs), how it was delivered and how any challenges were overcome. This gives a rounded, more engaging and interesting story that can help demonstrate the uniqueness of the work, and grounds any claims about outcomes and impacts in how this happened.

A strong foundation of evidence

Using the outcome- and impact-tracking approach outlined in this book builds a strong foundation of evidence from which to draw conclusions. If an initiative has been tracking outcomes against a pathway, and identifying data sources across it, then there is a strong basis to make claims about the wider impact of the work.

The Global Kids Online programme is a collaboration between the London School of Economics and Political Science and UNICEF that seeks to better understand the experiences of children online in different parts of the world. They wanted to learn how their work was making a difference to children and families.

We defined three pathways to impact for this work:

1. How the work of the project team inspires and supports people around the world to conduct their own research about children's experiences online.
2. How the partner countries contribute to changes in policy and practice locally to improve children's online experiences.
3. How the project team pulls together information from partner countries and uses this to influence the international agenda.

We were able to show how the work of the project – inspiring and supporting people to undertake research and develop partnerships in different countries, and policy influencing on the international stage – led to outcomes and impacts. These included policy and practice changes in partner countries, and influencing international bodies to better understand and include children's perspectives in their policies (Morton et al, 2019). Because there was evidence at every level of the pathways generated here, it was clear how this initiative, alongside other work, had contributed to children's safety online.

A compelling narrative

Using a theory of change – and, in particular, our headings – helps to create a compelling narrative of how an initiative made a difference to people or communities. These kinds of outcome reports might lead with a high-level outcome hook of some sort. In the Global Kids Online example, the report leads with the key contribution that 'Global Kids Online research has been used extensively to influence policy and practice in nine partner countries'.

Often when we facilitate workshops and events, we encourage participants to use our headings to tell the story of their work. Because the headings ask 'what you did', there are opportunities to explain the work. But because the headings ask to explain how people felt, what they learned and gained, what they did differently and what difference it makes, this establishes a structure for a much more compelling story.

Taking that final leap – from what people did differently to what difference does this make – is such a fundamental part of a strong contribution story. Even if it is difficult to strongly evidence that final step (because high-level outcomes are the ones most beyond our control), then thinking about them, and discussing and reporting on them, gives that sense of vision we discussed in Chapter 4 that is so important to driving this kind of complex work forward and keeping everyone on track.

Being able to claim a contribution to more children being safer online was essential to the contribution story of Global Kids Online, even though counting the number of children was not possible in a robust way. Instead, by being able to point to specific examples of children being safer, anchored in the overall contribution story, strong claims of contribution could be made.

Focus on the most important contribution made

An outcome map and pathway also creates a framework for identifying and emphasising the most important contribution that any initiative can and did make. Being clear about the most important contribution across the headings is a helpful way of focusing data collection, analysis and then, of course, reporting.

For example, a learning or knowledge sharing initiative might want to focus on reporting on learning outcomes, and acknowledge that outcomes beyond that (behaviour change or wider outcomes) are completely beyond their control. The focus of an outcome report would be on those learning outcomes (what they learned and gained), with the other outcomes symbolically on the map to demonstrate the potential contribution of the work.

For all of these reasons, using this framework for reporting gives an overall structure and scaffolding for any reporting. We also wanted to share our learning on the practical things that help make great reports.

Practical tips for great reporting

There are many resources and help guides for good reporting, and some of these are included in the resources section in Chapter 11. Here, we briefly outline some of the tips we regularly share with clients when helping with reports.

Components of an outcome- or impact-focused report

Our reports are structured around pathways and framed with context. The components of these reports include:

- an introduction to the work, its aims and objectives;
- a section setting out the context for the work;
- an illustration of the pathways;
- a description of the methods used, including data collection;
- analysis of the work for each of the items on the outcome map and/or at the step level (what we do, who with, and so on), using images, graphs and data visualisation where appropriate;
- risks and assumptions and how these have been experienced and addressed during the work;
- conclusions that draw together the findings from the work.

These components situate the work well in the context, and provide enough detail and robustness for a reader to understand the contribution of the work. There are other things that also help to make any report robust.

Tips for robust reporting

1. Describe your activities succinctly – they are fundamental, but the reader needs to know 'what next?'
2. Include discussion of the challenges and opportunities that were encountered during delivery – these help to put the work in context and bring it to life.
3. Answer the questions: who was engaged, how did they feel or react, what did they learn and gain, what did they do differently and what difference did this make?
4. Provide as much evidence as necessary to substantiate your claims.
5. Think carefully about who your report is for and write for them.
6. Use pictures, quotes and data visualisations to help tell the story.

Showing 'enough' evidence for the work

This is very subjective: what counts as 'enough' and 'good enough' evidence is highly variable depending on the initiative, audience and setting. Things like the data cultures we outlined in Chapter 3, the demands of funders and any specific reporting requirements all need to be considered. Some of the analysis discussion in the previous chapter can help figure out what this might look like for any specific example. Our advice would be to spend time thinking about this as part of any evaluation journey so that when it is time for reporting, it has already been agreed.

Reporting well on different parts of a contribution story

Here are our tips for reporting different levels of outcomes and impacts across maps and pathways.

Reporting on activities: 'what we do'

It should be easy to evidence and be confident in the column that explains 'what we do', but it can be a struggle to put into words how a programme or initiative has been delivered and what has changed over time. This is the anchor of a contribution story and an essential foundation for making claims about higher level outcomes and impacts.

- Explain what was done. Use pictures or other images – it's great to actually see people engaged in activities!
- Record what went well, what the challenges were and how these were overcome.
- Numbers might be relevant, such as the number of sessions delivered.
- Start as soon as possible, then refine and update the description as the project progresses, otherwise it can be easy to forget over time why things have been done this way.

Reporting on engagement: 'who with'

Who is being engaged and involved is the core of work seeking people-based change. We believe that it makes for a stronger and clearer contribution story if there is a separation between what was delivered ('what we did') and who was engaged and involved ('who with').

Reporting here offers some nice opportunities for quantitative data, graphs and numbers. It can be good to record who came in terms of types of people, numbers of sessions, repeat returners, social media and web stats, or the reach of the programme. These are the things that lend themselves to traditional quantitative data visualisation like graphs or pie charts.

While it is easy to emphasise these numbers, it is important to also tell the story of how a programme or initiative engaged people. For many initiatives, a lot of effort would have gone into ensuring that the people that were involved were the right people, were the intended recipients of whatever work was being planned and were engaged throughout the work where appropriate.

- How were the right people identified for this work?
- What was done to ensure they knew about the programme or initiative so they could engage?
- What hurdles to engagement were overcome?
- What were the key risks around engagement, and did they materialise?
- How were activities designed and delivered to ensure they were engaging for the intended recipients?

Reporting on reactions: 'how they feel'

Understanding people's reactions to any initiative is important as it is rolled out, and can help place the contribution of the work by understanding and demonstrating what it was that enabled people to engage fully with the work. Quotes are really useful to show that the assumptions about reactions and how people felt were realised. If there was any learning from initial reactions, and then a change in approach based on this, it would be useful to discuss this in this section. Qualitative data will be the most essential form here and, as well as quotes, images of people being positively engaged will be useful. For example, if an assumption was that children feel 'this is fun', then showing them having fun is much more powerful than other kinds of feedback.

Reporting on 'what they learn and gain'

As discussed in Chapter 7, data for this step in the map might include formal feedback and assessment of learning outcomes from training, events or other inputs, as well as more informal reflections on what people have learned from an initiative. When reporting these levels of outcomes, it is helpful to focus specifically on the extent to which the learning outcomes were realised, and if any unexpected outcomes emerged.

Reporting on 'what they do differently'

This step in outcome maps and pathways varies so hugely based on the specific initiative and focus that it is hard to generalise.

However, following the specific items on a pathway, and talking to risks and assumptions is vital. This level of outcome can lend itself to many forms of data visualisation depending on the data being used. Sometimes videos of people talking about what they are doing differently and what difference it makes can be a nice way of highlighting these changes.

Reporting on 'what difference does it make?'

It is hardest to report on what difference has been made and this is the part that is most difficult to evidence. There are a few approaches that can help here. Some people don't report on this step at all, but use this part of their map to highlight what is important in the long term. This means holding these high-level outcomes and impacts in a more symbolic way, and demonstrating the logic of their contribution up to that point. Others provide evidence to show some contribution to high-level outcomes, as described above for Global Kids Online. They cannot demonstrate that children are safer online across the world, but can show how they are likely to be safer in some instances. The language of contribution is so important here. If work has been commissioned under a government or funder outcome of improving wellbeing for the population, then all any single initiative can show is how they *contribute* to that high-level outcome. That might mean showing the people that have been directly influenced have improved wellbeing, or a policy has changed that expects to lead to improved wellbeing.

Sometimes it is good to lead with this level in impact reporting – bringing the outcomes or impacts defined here up to the front of a report to show what matters. This can be especially effective if this level of impacts is not being directly assessed.

Being honest about challenges

The best impact and outcome reports are not just shiny stories of the amazing achievements of initiatives. Complex people-based change is difficult, and if it has been evaluated, that is probably because success is neither obvious nor guaranteed. Sharing the difficulties along the way, and how these have been addressed, makes the story much more real and believable, as well as offering opportunities for others to learn.

- Describe any challenges, learning and adaptation.
- Include any careful work done in targeting the right people and rethinking problems.
- Explain what was going on in the wider context and how this helped or hindered the work – drawing on a contextual analysis, as in Chapter 5, can be useful for this.
- Explain and report on the risks and assumptions and how you worked with them throughout.

Bring it to life

Using graphics, stories, quotes and case studies brings reports to life. In Chapter 8 we set out how to use data well to draw conclusions. For reporting, this is about deciding what data to share and where this can add interest and insight to your contribution story.

Graphics can include photos, pictures, graphs, data visualisation and drawings. Chapter 11 shares some resources for creating these.

Using quotes well means pulling out ones that really illustrate the story and setting them in context so the reader can understand who said it and who they represent in the overall story. Again, bringing these voices in really helps the reader see the impact of the work.

Case studies can focus on a person, project, place or specific initiative and are a way of highlighting the more general points being made in the wider report. You can read more about this on the Matter of Focus website in our insight posts on case studies and bringing voices to reporting that are signposted in the resources section in Chapter 11.

Taking reporting forward

This chapter has set out reasons to focus on outcomes and impacts when reporting, and some of the challenges of that work. We hope you agree that reporting is best when it is a dynamic and interactive process of learning and improvement, rather than just a one-off effort for external audiences. Building up evidence and reporting internally before externally can help you get started on a process of layering and sense making that will mean a great report whoever the external audience is.

This approach encourages initiatives to pick up on the issues outlined in Chapter 4, and tell the strongest story they can of where they make the best contribution to the issues that matter to them. Setting it in context and acknowledging the work of partners and collaborators is part of that approach.

Our plea to you is just as in other chapters of this book: start somewhere – pull together your evidence and analysis and get going with reporting. Once you start to see your reports come to life, it will be clear where to improve and enhance them.

Try it yourself

Here are a few ways to get into an outcome- and impact-reporting mindset:

- Discuss your strongest impact story against each of our headings, or an outcome map if you have one. This might be something you have done in the past – a 'success story' – or work that you are undertaking now.
- Review a recent report of your work with an outcome and impact mindset: are you clear what difference this work made? Is the story of how you made a difference clearly articulated?
- Review your organisation's website with an impact mindset. How are you reporting on activities? Is there a balance of activity and impact information in how you present your work? What evidence do you provide?

10

Using this approach in different contexts and sectors

Throughout this book we have set out an approach to outcome and impact evaluation that works for the complex problems and issues that public services face. We have used this approach when working with clients from settings such as health, social work and care, policy, international development, research, and children and adult services. What we have found is that there is more in common across these contrasting sectors and contexts than divides them in relation to outcome and impact evaluation. Whatever the setting, the key challenges remain: how to work well with complex contexts; how to understand and work well with outcomes and impacts; how to get the relevant data, evidence and feedback; and how to embed this in day-to-day work.

This approach is for people who really *want* and need to understand and evidence the changes they are making and want to learn and improve as well as be able to showcase their work.

In this chapter we will explore some of the issues that often arise when working in this meaningful way with outcome and impact evaluation. We will discuss:

- organisations and settings using this approach;
- embedding outcome and impact tracking as a change process;

- practical tips for your outcome- and impact-evaluation journey;
- case studies: embedding outcome and impact tracking in organisations.

We hope you will finish this chapter with a sense of what is needed to steer the change process in any particular setting so that you can reap the rewards and benefits of really understanding the difference any work makes.

Organisations and settings using this approach

When we were planning this chapter, we liked the idea of creating a neat diagram that encapsulated all of the types of organisations and settings that find this approach useful and helpful. Once we started mapping that out, it quickly became clear that it wouldn't be possible, or at least, wouldn't make things any clearer. So, what is set out below is an overview of the reasons, sectors, approaches and types of work where we know outcome mapping and tracking is a great way to understand, evidence and report on change.

Outcome and impact mapping and tracking

Refer back to Figure 1.1 in Chapter 1 as a quick reminder about the types of initiatives we know this approach works well for.

Embedding outcome and impact tracking as a change process

In Chapter 1 we suggested that working towards new thinking for public services requires the meanings, capabilities and tools required to make the shift. Embedding outcome and impact tracking into organisations, systems and programmes is part of this bigger shift. It's not something that can happen quickly and it can be helpful to think of it as a change process. That means acknowledging that this work isn't easy. Embracing it as a change process, rather than a quick fix, helps to understand why it is hard, and to be satisfied with small steps along the change path.

Working meaningfully with outcomes, impact, data and evidence will throw up issues for most teams and organisations. Seeing these issues as part of a journey towards being a learning organisation, and to being able to understand and work well with complex change, is useful. Rather than seeing these issues as barriers and problems, embracing them as milestones on the journey is a much more positive mindset, and can help bring people along. These are some of the issues we most commonly observe people needing to tackle along the way.

Facing common issues

There are several common issues that occur when embracing this approach.

Are these the right outcomes?

Outcome and impact mapping poses challenges if the outcomes aren't right for an organisation or initiative. This might include outcome drift – where chasing funding has led to funders' outcomes usurping organisational ones. In other cases, there have been more and more outcomes added (usually to chase funding) and there is a lack of clarity, or disagreement, about what are the most important ones. The original aims of an initiative may express outcomes quite differently from current work. These issues are discussed in more detail in Chapter 4. The point here is that spending time looking at and thinking about the outcomes and impacts that are important to any initiative is hugely worthwhile but might throw up questions about outcomes that take time to get fixed.

Are activities aligned to outcomes?

We have worked with several teams who realise through outcome mapping that what they are planning to deliver really won't help work towards the outcomes that are important to them. Great! It's much better to realise this than to carry on with the work and worry later why results aren't as anticipated. But it is a stumbling block, and time is needed to rework activities and/or outcomes, to renegotiate with stakeholders and funders and get back on track.

Where is the data?

Most organisations don't have a clear picture of their data, feedback and evidence. They don't know what they have, and they don't know where it is. This is discussed in more detail in Chapters 3 and 7, which look at the data cultures that shape practice, and some of the practicalities of working well with data and evidence. Again, depending on what is uncovered when initiatives start trying to align data with their outcome or impact map, then there might be a lot of work to do. This might include streamlining, reorganising and reprioritising data and feedback collection. It will involve getting people engaged and involved in a data improvement journey, so winning hearts and minds will be necessary. Like other aspects of the shift, it will be a journey of data improvement, and can't happen overnight. But getting data sorted out so it is usable and available for learning, improvement and reporting is a big prize worth working towards.

Getting the skills and capacity

We have already described the skills and capacities needed by leaders, data and evidence people and others to work more meaningfully with outcome and impact tracking. These include leaders committed to a new way of working and to embedding evaluation, people who can work with data, evidence and feedback, and the capacity to undertake this work with a view to it saving time and resources later down the line. If an organisation doesn't have the skills and capacities needed, then another part of the journey will be to build these into the change process. It might mean skilling existing staff and engaging new ones, and will take time and effort.

Drivers for embedding outcome and impact evaluation

We have worked with many organisations on their journey to being outcome focused and data savvy. We have tried different

Figure 10.1: Pathway for embedding outcome and impact evaluation

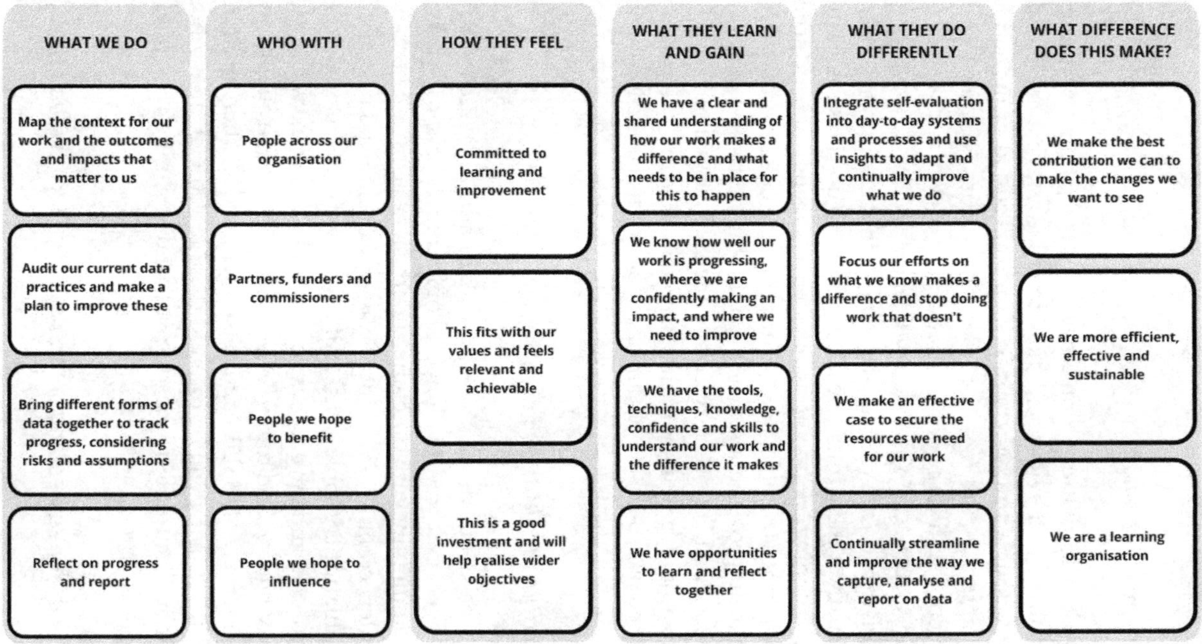

WHAT WE DO	WHO WITH	HOW THEY FEEL	WHAT THEY LEARN AND GAIN	WHAT THEY DO DIFFERENTLY	WHAT DIFFERENCE DOES THIS MAKE?
Map the context for our work and the outcomes and impacts that matter to us	People across our organisation	Committed to learning and improvement	We have a clear and shared understanding of how our work makes a difference and what needs to be in place for this to happen	Integrate self-evaluation into day-to-day systems and processes and use insights to adapt and continually improve what we do	We make the best contribution we can to make the changes we want to see
Audit our current data practices and make a plan to improve these	Partners, funders and commissioners	This fits with our values and feels relevant and achievable	We know how well our work is progressing, where we are confidently making an impact, and where we need to improve	Focus our efforts on what we know makes a difference and stop doing work that doesn't	We are more efficient, effective and sustainable
Bring different forms of data together to track progress, considering risks and assumptions	People we hope to benefit	This is a good investment and will help realise wider objectives	We have the tools, techniques, knowledge, confidence and skills to understand our work and the difference it makes	We make an effective case to secure the resources we need for our work	We are a learning organisation
Reflect on progress and report	People we hope to influence		We have opportunities to learn and reflect together	Continually streamline and improve the way we capture, analyse and report on data	

approaches to support the journey and observed different practices. We have created the pathway below to demonstrate this journey that client organisations undertake.

Drawing from our experience, it seems that there are key factors that help make this work. These include:

- **Having funders and stakeholders on board.** Where funders are interested in a meaningful approach to outcomes and impacts, and stakeholders value the approach, then it is much easier to work in this way. If the authorising environment values more traditional approaches, or data cultures are more reductionist, then it will be harder to achieve the changes needed for this new way of working.
- **Allocating resources.** Organisations that have research or data capability and capacity, and give everyone involved the time to do this work, including embracing reflection and learning, will find the journey easier.
- **Being committed to understanding if you are making a difference.** This is not a quick fix or a way of presenting a shiny story of impact. There are much easier ways of doing that! This approach is for people who really want and need to understand and evidence the changes they are making and want to learn and improve as well as be able to showcase their work.
- **Orientation as a learning organisation.** Organisations that have this orientation tend to fare better when embedding outcome and impact tracking. That means:

  [O]rganizations where people continually expand their capacity to create the results they truly desire, where new and expansive patterns of thinking are nurtured, where collective aspiration is set free, and where people are continually learning to see the whole together. (Senge, 1990: 3)

- **Drivers pushing towards the new thinking about public services.** Whether it is the policy, practice or wider environment, if there is an acknowledgement of the importance of the new thinking for public services, data and evidence, and working with outcomes, as we discuss in Chapters 2 to 4, then it will be easier to make the case for the work.

Practical tips for your outcome- and impact-evaluation journey

We have set out some of the tricky issues and wider factors that are important to embedding this way of working in any initiative or organisation. We hope we haven't put you off! There are many practical things organisations can do to get on the journey, and each step means that they will be in a better place than before:

- **Do a bit at a time.** Throughout this book our plea has been to just get going. Taking the journey step by step: defining outcomes and impacts; aligning and improving data; tracking, reporting and learning; making the case. These are all activities that are mutually reinforcing and can be started on a small scale and rolled out over time.
- **Keep it live.** It can be difficult if momentum is lost, so keeping the process live for everyone involved makes it much easier. That means having a plan for how the work will be taken forward, bringing it to routine meetings, allocating team time to review and refine. Doing a little every week or month is a lot easier than allocating less frequent, larger chunks of time.
- **Spread the approach.** Starting small can help but spreading the approach across an organisation also means that the culture starts to shift and everyone gets on board.
- **Make data everyday.** Data collection and analysis can be streamlined into everyday interactions, reviewed at team or other scheduled meetings, and reported on within organisational reporting cycles. Making data collection, analysis and reporting part of the everyday life of an organisation helps to embed evaluative mindsets and focus on what matters.
- **People drive change.** Getting everyone on board with the outcome- and impact-evaluation journey, and being clear on what role they need to play, makes this work easier. That

means everyone knows why they are doing this, what data they need to collect, how they should record things, what analysis will be shared, and the vision for the difference the work will make to the people and communities they care about.

- **Bring meaning and fun to work!** Organisations we support who bring people into all aspects of the process have the best success. That might be through collective analysis sessions (with cake!), where a group considers the emerging data. It might be through designing creative and appropriate feedback mechanisms that really work for the context of the initiative. It might be in reviewing reports and considering to what extent the work is making a difference. On the whole, people find it inspiring and empowering to really consider what difference they are making to the people and communities they care about.

Case studies: embedding outcome and impact tracking in organisations

Outcome tracking for new and innovative ways of working

Future Pathways supports adult survivors of in-care child abuse in Scotland. They wanted to be able to demonstrate their contribution in a highly politicised area of work, with beneficiaries who have extensive vulnerabilities and overlapping issues. Taking the approach described in this book has enabled them to embed evaluation, demonstrating to people using the service and the government that the person-centred approach to the work is effective (and cost effective). They have embedded collective analysis sessions in their outcome tracking work to help facilitate this – bringing staff together to reflect on data and track outcomes in OutNav.

Outcome tracking across a small organisation

WHALE Arts is a small community art organisation in the north of Edinburgh. They started using the approach as part of some work funded by the intermediary body for community health (Edinburgh Community Health Forum). Having been through the process for one project, they could see how this approach and software could help them track outcomes across their whole organisation. With some extra facilitation, they mapped out all of their workstreams. They felt that this process helped them to own their own outcomes rather than following funder outcomes.

> 'I believe [this approach] has the possibility to be transformational in terms of how we collect, store and use data, what we consider data, and also how we report to funders and decide which funds to apply to ... I hope it will move us away from thinking about our data only in relation to what we report to funders. I think that too many third sector orgs collect data for their funders and not for themselves. I've been calling this "owning our outcomes".' (Leah Black, Chief Executive, WHALE Arts)

Outcome and impact tracking for a research organisation

Health Technology Wales started using this approach when they were established, as they realised the importance of demonstrating their impact and the return on investment as a new national body. They were established by the Welsh government to review health technologies and make recommendations about adoption for the NHS and social care in Wales. They had quantitative researchers and economists on the team, but no qualitative researchers. They established outcome maps for each main area of work and tracked progress.

HTW Director Susan Myles believes this approach has helped the sustainability of the organisation: "I think the impact work has helped in demonstrating our contributions and giving confidence to further invest in HTW." In 2021 they were also awarded the International Network of Agencies for Health Technology Assessment (INAHTA) Impact award, voted on by 50+ health technology agencies from across the world.

Conclusion

This chapter has illustrated that the approach outlined in this book is appropriate and helpful across a wide range of sectors and settings. As long as the work is complex, and is about people-based change, then it can be helpful. It can be applied to small projects, programmes, organisations, research initiatives and partnerships – with the required resources mirroring the extent of the ambition.

We have set out some of the pointers we often give to the people we work with about facing the tricky issues, and practical tips to get going and keep going. One of the most rewarding aspects of our work is to see clients really embrace the approach, make it their own, and share their learning from having gone on the journey to being more outcome and impact savvy.

We hope you have recognised your own work experience in the sectors and settings we have described in this short chapter.

11

Becoming an outcome- and impact-focused organisation

We asked some of the organisations and teams we work with to share their insights into the way of working we have set out in this book. This chapter shares their thoughts, resources they find helpful, and other resources we often recommend. We also explain the software OutNav, which we have developed to support the approach.

We would like to acknowledge Richard Darke, Edinburgh & Lothians Greenspace Trust; Julie Gardner, Thistle Foundation; Eleanor MacKillop, Wales Centre for Public Policy; Gill Toms, Bangor University; Catriona Windle, Health All Round; and Alex Perry, Helen Berry, Grace Robertson and Simon Bradstreet from Matter of Focus for their suggestions.

Advice from other organisations on the journey

Stick with the messy, emergent stuff over the first few months because you will gradually get a handle on things and a plan will start to take shape. But this does require several meetings and thinking space, so time needs to be allocated. I would also recommend trying to include all the important voices right from the start.

It will take time to develop your map and pathways.

If possible, use the approach to think about impact before it happens – as you are developing a project.

Be pragmatic about collecting data – the more it is built into everyday practice, the easier it will be.

Try out new methods (like reflective impact logs) on specific projects and then see whether they can be rolled out more widely.

Start trying to weave a narrative into tracking early on. Once the narrative is taking shape, it is easier to think about the outcomes and how to capture them – how to make the story convincing.

Present your emerging impact to management committees and trustees.

It's a great way of presenting your organisation's achievements. Before, everything just got lost in the annual plethora of funding reports – now, it's much more dynamic than an annual report and more impressive.

It takes time to embed the discipline of this approach into your work, but we are committed to doing so and it very much informs how we think and plan.

Resources to help with evaluation thinking

AMEC taxonomy of evaluation

This taxonomy table breaks down public communication into several stages such as inputs, outputs and impacts, and suggests ways to think analytically about each stage. Useful if you need to evaluate the effectiveness of your PR or communications strategy.

https://amecorg.com/amecframework/home/supporting-material/
  taxonomy/

Matter of Focus headings

An introduction to using our outcome- and impact-mapping headings.

https://www.matter-of-focus.com/using-our-headings/

Matter of Focus insight posts

A wide-ranging collection of articles, case studies and videos covering topics across different stages of the evaluation journey, including tips for outcome mapping, data collection, bringing voices to your story, analysis and reporting.

https://www.matter-of-focus.com/insights/

Most Significant Change

The Most Significant Change (MSC) approach involves generating and analysing personal accounts of change and deciding which of these accounts is the most significant – and why.

https://www.betterevaluation.org/en/plan/approach/most_significant
_change

Resources to help with data collection

Digital survey tools

There are several digital survey tools out there. At Matter of Focus, we prefer SmartSurvey because data is held in the UK. Our rationale is here:

https://www.matter-of-focus.com/feedback-matters-choosing-the-
right-survey-tool/
https://www.smartsurvey.co.uk/

Evaluation Support Scotland

There are lots of useful resources and information on this website. In particular, we find the mapping tools and templates great for data collection. Look for mapping resources – body map, journey map, relationship map.

https://evaluationsupportscotland.org.uk/resources

Identity boxes

An introduction to the idea of identity boxes as a method of data collection.

https://www.nicole-brown.co.uk/identity-boxes/

Online form tools

Online form tools such as Google Forms and Microsoft Office Forms allow users to create and share surveys. This is useful for gathering feedback from clients and other groups you engage with.

https://docs.google.com/forms
https://forms.office.com/

Quick feedback tools

A quick way to gather data online or face to face using a QR code or via a link. Both Mentimeter and Vevox offer a freemium product, where you can use the basic version without paying.

https://www.mentimeter.com/
https://www.vevox.com/

Reflective impact log

A template developed by Matter of Focus to collect reflections from those involved in service delivery, which can then be used as evidence in your evaluation.

https://www.matter-of-focus.com/3-feedback-tools/

Researchfish

A platform that uses technology and algorithms to collect outcomes and outputs of research from the web, external data sources and the researchers themselves. They also offer bespoke consultancy services to support you to interpret, evaluate and apply data to inform strategy development and future research decisions.

https://researchfish.com/

Overton

Overton is the world's largest searchable index of policy documents, guidelines, think tank publications and working papers. They parse each document, finding references, people and key concepts, and then link them to the relevant news stories, academic research, think tank output and other policy. A paid service allows people to search these documents and see where ideas, papers, reports and staff are being cited or mentioned.

https://www.overton.io/

Twitter analytics

Allows Twitter users to see data on engagement with their tweets. Useful for demonstrating the reach of your social media accounts.

https://analytics.twitter.com/

Warwick-Edinburgh Mental Wellbeing Scales (WEMWBS)

Allows people to scale themselves in terms of coping and confidence. This is used at different points in the process of working with people, giving them an insight into where they are, and as a way of capturing the person's journey.

https://warwick.ac.uk/fac/sci/med/research/platform/wemwbs/

Resources to help with embedding the approach

Active Implementation Hub

If you are working on a new challenge or implementing a new programme, project or service, then there are some helpful resources and thinking tools here.

https://nirn.fpg.unc.edu/module-4/introduction

Centre for Public Impact

Lots of helpful resources on the kind of organisational and governance practices that support a move to more complexity informed and learning approaches. In particular, those on the Human Learning Systems mini site.

https://www.centreforpublicimpact.org

https://www.centreforpublicimpact.org/partnering-for-learning/human-learning-systems

Evaluation Support Scotland – Leadership in Evaluation Enquiry Report

This research identifies the key skills, qualities and capabilities for staff that promote successful leadership on evaluation within organisations.

https://evaluationsupportscotland.org.uk/resources/leadership-in-evaluation-enquiry-report/

Learning organisations

A useful summary of the theory and practice of learning organisations, as defined by Peter Senge.

https://infed.org/peter-senge-and-the-learning-organization/

Miro

An online whiteboard tool, great for collaborating with your team at various stages of the process. We often use it for data audits and for beginning the outcome mapping process.

https://miro.com/

Personal outcomes

Designed for service delivery organisations looking to orientate their systems and processes to what matters to the people they support, the Personal Outcomes Network website is full of useful resources, including on meaningful recording of outcomes.

https://personaloutcomes.network/

Reflective models

A quick introduction to various reflective models. Further examples can be found in the related posts section on the website.

https://www.nicole-brown.co.uk/reflective-model-according-to-rolfe/
https://www.nicole-brown.co.uk/reflective-model-according-to-gibbs/

Resources to help with reporting

Canva

An online design tool, great for creating engaging graphics to include in your reports.

https://www.canva.com/

OutNav – a system for embedding meaningful outcome and impact evaluation

We set up our company, Matter of Focus, and built our software platform, OutNav, because we knew this way of working brought meaning and helped address some of the challenges that people faced when trying to make a difference. We believe in supporting people to do this job well, but we also observed that there weren't any tools and, in particular, software that made this easier.

While you don't need OutNav to adopt this approach, over the years we have found that using OutNav helps with the issues we have set out in this chapter in the following ways:

- OutNav holds outcome maps and pathways and enables data and evidence to be allocated to different parts of a pathway. Outcome tracking happens through analysis within the software, along with colour coding of confidence and progress – leading to colour outcome maps that give a visual picture of where the initiative is in terms of progress and where data need to be improved.
- This is a collaborative process, with users able to log in to a single outcome map and track it together, regardless of their organisation affiliation. Users can log in, see what others have done and do their own part of the work.
- We have described the issues with data improvement, of bringing disparate data together, and analysis in previous chapters. OutNav breaks the process into manageable chunks – creating discrete units of analysis across pathways. It is much easier to follow the advice we have been giving of 'just get started somewhere' with these manageable chunks set out in this way.
- OutNav enables report sharing direct from the software to people within and outside organisations.
- OutNav can be used to plot and link different outcome and impact areas across an organisation.

See www.outnav.net for more information.

References

Ahmed, I.K. and Dantata, B.S. (2016) 'Problems and challenges of policy implementation for national development', *Research on Humanity and Social Sciences*, 6(15): 60–65.

Archibald, T., Sharrock, G., Buckley, J. and Cook, N. (2016) 'Assumptions, conjectures, and other miracles: The application of evaluative thinking to theory of change models in community development', *Evaluation and Program Planning*, 59: 119–127.

Australian Government (2019) 'Delivering for Australians. A world-class Australian public service: The government's APS reform agenda', *Department of the Prime Minister and Cabinet* [online] 13 December. Available from: https://www.pmc.gov.au/resource-centre/government/delivering-for-australians [Accessed 4 October 2021].

Bicket, M., Christie, I., Gilbert, N., Hills, D., Penn, A. and Wilkinson, H. (2020) *Magenta Book 2020: Supplementary Guide: Handling Complexity in Policy Evaluation*, London: HM Treasury.

Black, L. (2021) 'Funding Utopia' [online]. Available from: https://leah-black.medium.com/funding-utopia-2-ten-fifteen-years-unrestricted-outcomes-community-wealth-and-more-b32760b32dd3 [Accessed 15 March 2022].

Blamey, A. and Mackenzie, M. (2007) 'Theories of change and realistic evaluation: Peas in a pod or apples and oranges?', *Evaluation*, 13(4): 439–455.

Bozarth, J.D. (2013) 'Unconditional positive regard', in M. Cooper, M. O'Hara, P.F. Schmid and A.C. Bohart (eds) *The Handbook of Person-Centred Psychotherapy and Counselling*, New York: Palgrave Macmillan/Springer Nature, pp 180–192.

Cameron, W.B. (1969) Informal Sociology: A casual introduction to sociological thinking, New York: Random House.

CECAN – Centre for Evaluating Complexity Across the Nexus (2020) 'Supplementary Guide: Handling complexity in policy evaluation', HM Treasury [online]. Available from: https://www.cecan.ac.uk/news/handling-complexity-in-policy-evaluation-magenta-book-2020-supplementary-guide/ [Accessed 4 October 2021].

Christie, C. (2011) 'Christie Commission on the future delivery of public services', Scottish Government [online] 29 June. Available from: https://www.gov.scot/publications/commission-future-delivery-public-services/ [Accessed 4 October 2021].

Cook, A. (2015) 'Partnership working across UK public services: Evidence review', Edinburgh: What Works Scotland [online]. Available from: http://whatworksscotland.ac.uk/wp-content/uploads/2015/12/WWS-Evidence-Review-Partnership-03-Dec-2015-.pdf [Accessed 7 October 2021].

Cook, A. (2017) 'Outcome based approaches in public service reform', Edinburgh: What Works Scotland [online]. Available from: http://whatworksscotland.ac.uk/wp-content/uploads/2017/04/OutcomeBasedApproachesinPublicServiceReform.pdf [Accessed 25 February 2022].

Cook, A. and Miller, E. (2012) *Talking Points Personal Outcomes Approach: A practical guide for organisations*, Edinburgh: Joint Improvement Team, Scottish Government.

Crawford, C., Edwards, A., Farquharson, C., Greaves, E., Trevelyan, G., Wallace, E. and White, C. (2016) *Magic Breakfast: Evaluation report and executive summary*, London: The Education Endowment Foundation.

Crewe, E. and Young, J. (2002) *Bridging Research and Policy: Context, evidence and links*, London: Overseas Development Institute.

Darnton, A. and Horne, J. (2013) 'Influencing behaviours – moving beyond the individual: ISM user guide', Scottish Government [online]. Available from: https://www.gov.scot/publications/influencing-behaviours-moving-beyond-individual-user-guide-ism-tool/ [Accessed 1 March 2022].

Davies, H.T. and Nutley, S.M. (2000) 'Healthcare: Evidence to the fore', in H.T. Davies, S.M. Nutley and P.C. Smith (eds) *What Works: Evidence-based policy and practice in public services*, Bristol: Policy Press, pp 43–67.

Gabbay, J. and le May, A. (2004) 'Evidence based guidelines or collectively constructed "mindlines?" Ethnographic study of knowledge management in primary care', *BMJ*, 329: 1013 https://doi.org/10.1136/bmj.329.7473.1013

Garvin, D.A. (1993) 'Building a learning organization', *Harvard Business Review*, 71(4): 78–91 [online]. Available from: https://hbr.org/1993/07/building-a-learning-organization [Accessed 5 October 2021].

Glendinning, C., Clarke, S., Hare, P., Kitchetkova, I., Maddison, J. and Newbronner, L. (2006) *Outcomes-focused Services for Older People*, Bristol: Policy Press.

Government of Canada. 'Theory-based approaches to evaluation: Concept and practices' [online]. Available from: https://www.canada.ca/en/treasury-board-secretariat/services/audit-evaluation/evaluation-government-canada/theory-based-approaches-evaluation-concepts-practices.html [Accessed 5 October 2021].

Huff, D. and Geis, I. (1954) *How to Lie with Statistics*, New York: Norton.

Matter of Focus 'Understand the unique context of your work' [online]. Available from: https://www.matter-of-focus.com/understand-the-unique-context-of-your-work/ [Accessed 5 October 2021].

Matter of Focus '3 feedback tools to help you track your outcomes and impact' [online]. Available from: https://www.matter-of-focus.com/3-feedback-tools/ [Accessed 7 October 2021].

Mayne, J. (2008) 'Contribution analysis: An approach to exploring cause and effect', ILAC Brief 16, pp 1–4. Available from: https://hdl.handle.net/10568/70124 [Accessed 7 October 2021].

Miller, E. and Barrie, K. (2016) 'Learning from the Meaningful and Measurable Project: Strengthening links between identity, action and decision-making', Healthcare Improvement Scotland [online]. Available from: https://ihub.scot/media/2126/po-learning.pdf [Accessed 25 February 2022].

Montague, S. (2012) 'Theory-based approaches for practical evaluation' [online]. Available from: https://www.pmn.net/wp-content/uploads/Theory-based-Approaches-for-Practical-Evaluation.pdf [Accessed 5 October 2021].

Morton, S. (2012) *Exploring and Assessing Social Research Impact: A case study of a research partnership's impacts on policy and practice*, Edinburgh: University of Edinburgh.

Morton, S. (2015) 'Creating research impact: The roles of research users in interactive research mobilisation', *Evidence & Policy: A Journal of Research, Debate and Practice*, 11(1): 35–55.

Morton, S. and Casey, T. (2017) *Changing National Policy on Violence Affecting Children: An impact assessment of UNICEF and partners' multi-country study on the drivers of violence affecting children in Peru*, Edinburgh: University of Edinburgh.

Morton, S., Grant, A., Cook, A., Berry, H., McMellon, C., Robbin, M. and Ipince, A. (2019) *Children's Experiences Online: Building global understanding and action*, Innocenti [online]. Available from: https://www.unicef-irc.org/publications/1065-childrens-experiences-online-building-global-understanding-and-action.html [Accessed 7 October 2021].

National Performance Framework, Scottish Government website [online]. Available from: https://nationalperformance.gov.scot/ [Accessed 5 October 2021].

Needham, C. and Mangan, C. (2016) 'The 21st century public servant: Working at three boundaries of public and private', *Public Money and Management*, 36(4): 265–272.

Osborne, S. and Strokosch, K. (2013) 'It takes two to tango? Understanding the co-production of public services by integrating the services management and public administration perspectives', *British Journal of Management*, 24: 1–29.

Patton, M.Q. (2011) *Developmental Evaluation: Applying complexity concepts to enhance innovation and use*, New York: Guilford Press.

Public Health England (2019) 'Health matters: Whole systems approach to obesity', UK Government Publication [online] 25 July. Available from: https://www.gov.uk/government/publications/health-matters-whole-systems-approach-to-obesity/health-matters-whole-systems-approach-to-obesity [Accessed 4 October 2021].

Rogers, P.J. (2008) 'Using programme theory to evaluate complicated and complex aspects of interventions', *Evaluation*, 14(1): 29–48.

Saunders, B., Sim, J., Kingstone, T., Baker, S., Waterfield, J., Bartlam, B., Burroughs, H. and Jinks, C. (2018) 'Saturation in qualitative research: Exploring its conceptualization and operationalization', *Quality & Quantity*, 52(4): 1893–1907.

Schein, E.H. (1985) 'Defining organizational culture', *Classics of Organization Theory*, 3(1): 490–502.

Senge, P.M. (1990) *The Fifth Discipline*, New York: Random House Business.

Shove, E., Pantzar, M. and Watson, M. (2012) *The Dynamics of Social Practice: Everyday life and how it changes*, London: SAGE Publications Ltd.

Social Care Wales (2022) 'Friend not foe: Supporting meaningful outcomes focused recording in social care in Wales', Welsh Government [online]. Available from: https://socialcare.wales/cms_assets/file-uploads/Friend-not-Foe-English.pdf [Accessed 25 February 2022].

The Manchester Partnership (2021) 'Public Service Reform' [online]. Available from: https://www.manchester.gov.uk/manchesterpartnership/info/5/public_service_reform [Accessed 4 October 2021].

United Nations Sustainable Development Goals [online]. Available from: https://sdgs.un.org/ [Accessed 6 October 2021].

Weiss, C.H. (1998) *Evaluation: Methods for studying programs and policies*, Upper Saddle River, NJ: Prentice Hall.

Whitebloom, S. (2020) ' "Care" can and should work but it is a postcode lottery for young care leavers', *Oxford News Blog*, Oxford: University of Oxford website [online]. Available from: https://www.ox.ac.uk/news/arts-blog/care-can-and-should-work-it-postcode-lottery-young-care-leavers [Accessed 5 October 2021].

World Health Organization (2016) 'INSPIRE: 7 strategies to end violence against children' [online]. Available from: https://www.who.int/publications/i/item/inspire-seven-strategies-for-ending-violence-against-children [Accessed 7 October 2021].

Index

References to figures appear in *italic* type;
those in **bold** type refer to tables.

influence, as benefit of public
  service system evaluation 4
information management systems 8
innovation, and pathways 90
inputs 50, *50*
internal learning, reporting for 139,
  140, 141
International Network of Agencies
  for Health Technology
  Assessment (INAHTA) 160
ISM framework *64*, 64–65
  action for violence against
    children in Peru 71–74
  case studies 65–67
  risks and assumptions 69–70

K

knowledge 8

L

leadership 5, 7, 8, *8*
  in complex work 14, 24–25
Leadership in Evaluation Enquiry
  Report, Evaluation Support
  Scotland 167
learning
  capture of 52, 90
  embedding of into organisational
    practice 5, 7, 21
  reporting 139, *140*, 141, 148
  shift in thinking in public service
    systems 7, *8*
learning cycles 40
learning organisation 4, 40, 157
  resources for 167
Life Changes Trust 119, 124–125
lived experience, and data
  cultures 36
local government, multiple
  outcome frameworks 46
London School of Economics and
  Political Science 143
Lothian Minority Ethnic Health
  Inclusion Service 66

M

macro level of initiatives 62
making a difference *see* evaluation
  of public service systems
management
  in complexity 20–21

see also leadership
Mangan, C. 20
material factors in evaluation of
  public service systems 8–9
Matter of Focus 50, 150, 162
  insight posts 164
  outcome- and impact-mapping
    headings *82*, 82–84, 99,
    105–106, 144, 151, 163
  OutNav software 28, 162,
    168–169
  reflective impact log template 165
Mayne, John 25
Mentimeter 165
meso level of initiatives 62
micro level of initiatives 62
Microsoft Office Forms 165
Miro 167
mixed data 37–38, **38**, *38*, 104,
  133, **134**
  see also qualitative data;
    quantitative data
Montague, Steve 81
MSC (Most Significant Change)
  approach 164
multiple perspectives, in complex
  situations 21
My Life My Way project, East
  Renfrewshire Health and
  Social Care Partnership 66
Myles, Susan 160

N

Needham, C. 20
non-profit organisations, multiple
  outcome frameworks 46

O

online form tools 165
online whiteboard tools 167
organisations, outcome mapping
  for *95*, 95–96, 152–153
outcome or impact mapping 5,
  28, 76–78, *79*, 80–82, 98–99,
  100, 121–122, 134–135, 153,
  160–161
  advice and resources 162–169
  art of 98
  case studies 159–160
  characteristics of 84–86, *87*, 88
  common issues in 154–155

9 781447 361930